Easy Casino Gambling

Easy Casino Gambling
Winning Strategies for the Beginner

Gayle Mitchell

Skyhorse Publishing

www.skyhorsepublishing.com

10 9 8 7 6 5 4 3 2 1

Library of Congress Cataloging-in-Publication Data

Mitchell, Gayle.
Easy casino gambling : winning strategies for the beginner / Gayle Mitchell.
  p. cm.
  Includes bibliographical references and index.
  ISBN-13: 978-1-60239-011-9 (pbk. : alk. paper)
  ISBN-10: 1-60239-011-8 (pbk. : alk. paper)
  1. Gambling. 2. Casinos. I. Title.

GV1301.M57 2007
795--dc22
2006103308

Printed in Canada

To my mother, who enjoys the sound of "raining coins," and to Jim, my lifelong gambling and traveling partner

Table of Contents

Introduction

My casino gambling education began in 1990, when I first visited Las Vegas. Our son was driving along the Strip and, just before making a left onto Fremont Street, he announced, "Prepare to be blinded." And blinded we were, from the very first hotel all the way to Union Plaza's thousand lights at the end of the street. The excitement made my heart pound, and I laughed out loud. I could not wait to park so I could drink in all the thrills of Las Vegas.

I've often said that I want to see the world before I leave this earth, and my husband I and have traveled extensively. However, nothing I had seen before could have prepared me for the splendor and nonstop action of Las Vegas. It was pulsating, seductive. I couldn't imagine going to sleep. I just wanted to experience more of everything the city had to offer.

At Fitzgeralds I had my first slot machine experience. It was at a twenty-five-cent machine that took up to five coins. I played two quarters and hit the jackpot—$250.

Not bad for a beginner.

I would have won $1,000 if I had played just three more coins.

That was my first gambling lesson: Play maximum coins!

The roulette tables were like magnets. To this day, I cannot pass those glittering, spinning wheels without stopping to check out the action. At a quarter roulette table, I noticed a man tossing a chip in the air before every spin. Wherever the chip landed, that was his bet for the spin. I thought, "You call that a system?"

1

I wondered how many people really know what they're doing when they gamble.

Next I wandered by the blackjack table, where players sat intensely over their cards. Now, I was familiar with basic blackjack, but I did not know all the rules. So I made a mental note to brush up on the game and give it a shot another time.

I knew nothing about craps and baccarat. Video poker looked too complicated, so I played the slots only. Later, I found out that the slots is the game most Vegas gamblers play.

That first night of touring a Vegas casino touched off my curiosity. After that, I wanted to learn more about the full range of gambling options that casinos offer.

Recognizing that I was uneducated about gambling, I decided to go home, start reading, and begin practicing. I knew I would come back to Las Vegas, and I wanted to have even more fun the next time. I realized that I needed to educate myself. And I did just that!

I have read that there are more than eighty million regular casino gamblers, but that fewer than 2 percent are knowledgeable about percentages, rules, and basic techniques for playing casino games. Few of them know the best and worst bets in the casino.

When I read that statistic, I was amazed. I asked myself, "Why do so many people who are normally informed consumers throw away their hard-earned money on something they know so little about?"

These are the same people who clip coupons, comparison shop, and read consumer news reports just to save a few dollars and make informed product selections in their day-to-day lives. Yet they lose bundles at casinos simply because they do not take the time to do the most basic research.

As I studied casino games and learned about the enormous edge that the house has over the player in many casino bets, I determined to guide other casino gamblers "out of the woods." That determination led me to write books and present seminars to educate casino gamblers, so that they could make more intelligent and profitable gambling decisions. Gambling can be a great way to spend one's vacation, but it need not be a mental holiday!

There's more enjoyment involved in gambling when one understands the games.

I decided to dedicate a number of Web sites to improving gamblers' understanding of casino games. In the past, I have been editor of three on-line newsletters: *Slots Report, Bingo Showcase,* and *Casino Travel Showcase.* Currently, I am editor of Casino Players Ezine, an online newsletter. My goal was and is to increase the percentage of gamblers who understand basic odds and casino strategy.

To that end, this book concerns itself with casino games and bets where the house edge is no greater than 3 percent. I have deliberately avoided discussing inferior games and bets where the house edge is higher than this; if gamblers can avoid such bets, they will have profited immediately from this book!

Working with only the best bets in the house, this book clarifies the principles for reducing the house edge as much as possible, and it guides the reader in developing solid gambling strategies for the ten best casino games. It should be stated here that when the house edge is referred to, it has been calculated against optimal player strategy. The further you deviate from this, the greater the house's edge. The goal of this book is thus to teach the reader the pleasure and profitability of playing as close to optimally as possible.

As with any educational book for beginners, what's most important are the facts, and the facts explained clearly. I expect that readers of how-to gambling books will want to learn only those essentials—just the facts, ma'am—that will prepare them for the jungle out there or, in this case, for any casino. So I have tried to make this an easy, enjoyable read, and to keep the math, charts, and percentages to a minimum.

I have taken great pleasure in walking into a casino and knowing something about all of the major games. Knowing what the best games are and how to play them allows one the envious advantage of moving confidently from one game to another. This book encourages both an intelligent and a diversified approach to all that the casino offers. When you master the best games and use the lowest-cost strategies to play, you can enjoy your stay in any gaming location anywhere in the world.

And casinos are to be found the world over. For that reason, I've included a section on domestic and foreign casinos. I encourage my readers to expand their horizons beyond Las Vegas to include Atlantic City, Mississippi, Connecticut's Foxwoods, Canada, and international locations. If you are confident in your gambling skills, combining travel with a little action can lead to a great and even profitable travel experience.

Wherever they are, casinos normally "hold all the cards," so to speak, with high odds stacked against gamblers winning. There are ways, discussed in this book, to restack those odds in your favor. With short-term play, for example, the law of averages does not have time to kick in, and knowledgeable players who minimize the house edge while maximizing their odds have a great opportunity to walk away winners.

You don't have to be brainy or rich to take up the casino challenge in a fair fight. That's the beauty of the low-cost strategies you will discover in this book. The biggest differences among casino gamblers are not a matter of gender or age but of levels of "casino know-how." Here's one constant you can bet on: The intelligent, educated, prepared player will fare better than the uneducated gambler, and deservedly so!

This book is structured as a guided tour of the casino, visiting the ten best games one after another, and explaining the best basic strategies for playing each. Imagine that with each chapter we move to the next game, the next area of the casino. Summaries of the principal strategies and tips for each of these major casino games are gathered in the appendix at the end of the book.

In addition to discussing the games themselves, the book offers advice and information about such subjects as Wager Management, Comps, Internet Gambling, Casino Security, and the Dos and Don'ts of Gambling. Because a lot of the terminology used in and about casinos may be unfamiliar to beginning gamblers—often it sounds like a foreign language!—the book contains sections on gambling lingo.

However, before getting to the colorful languages of the games, and to the games themselves, let me begin with the basics of gambling, what I call the Four D's of better playing: Development, Dexterity, Discipline, and Diversification.

Reader, enjoy!

The Four D's of Intelligent Gambling

1

I like the expression "You don't have to work if you know how to play." Knowing how to play well takes four key ingredients, what I call the Four D's of intelligent gambling.

Here they are:

1. *Development* means education.

    An educated gambler knows the rules and percentages.

    Gamblers should not allow themselves to lose a single dollar without having at least some knowledge of the game they are playing. Don't let the casino be your classroom!

    An educated gambler knows when to quit! This means setting limits and sticking to them. (See "Wager Management," below).

2. *Dexterity* is your playing skill.

    Improving your skill and the range of games you can play should be fun, just as knowledgeable gambling is fun. You get more for your money when you are a skilled player.

    You get the satisfaction of knowing that you practiced the right strategies to get the best playing bargain.

3. *Discipline* conjures up images of school days, homework, final exams, exercise, eating right . . . oh my!

We don't like to think about discipline, especially in terms of leisure activities.

But discipline can be a gambler's best friend.

It's what separates the winners from the losers.

Recently, after my brother-in-law returned from a trip to Las Vegas, I asked him the usual question: "Did you win?" And he gave the usual reply: "Well, yeah, but it was the same old story. I didn't know when to stop and kept on playing."

Doesn't that sound familiar?

Discipline doesn't have to be difficult. Prove it to yourself by trying this advice just once and seeing what happens. If you lose a few bets in a row, walk away. Use the same strategy on the next game.

You'll see that this is not so hard.

Discipline is easier to take in small doses, and in the long run, a disciplined player's winnings are more satisfying because that player relies on more than just pure luck. He or she has worked at winning and had a good time doing it too.

4. Diversification is my favorite D.

It means learning and practicing all of the best games in a casino.

You will discover great satisfaction in knowing that when one of these games lets you down—and they all will, at one time or another—you will have other choices.

Wager Management

2

Before you learn about any of the best casino games and the playing strategies for each, and before you leave for that next gambling trip, you must have a plan . . . a winning plan.

The key component of any such plan is wager management.

Without wager management, you literally put yourself at the mercy of the casinos. And the casinos have no mercy.

The casino management may seem like friendly folks, and they may be friendly folks, but they will smile at you as the house pockets your last dime.

Wager management takes the control away from the casino and keeps it where it belongs—in your hands. A winning wager-management plan whittles away at the casino's greatest edge: the player's lack of self-control.

So, what exactly is wager management?

It's a plan you make before your gambling trip. In this plan, you decide what you will spend, how big your bets will be, and when you will quit playing.

If you decide that gambling will be more than an occasional holiday in which you accept defeat in advance, I recommend that you open a separate bank account and record and detail each gambling trip by date and number of days.

Start by deciding on your total bankroll for your trip—the amount you can afford to spend. Notice that I said "spend," not "lose." A winning attitude is part of your winning plan. Next, you need to decide how you will divide your total bankroll over the course of your stay. Then you should determine which games you will play and how you will manage your wagers for each of those games.

Let's look at a sample wager-management plan.

Suppose you decide on $1,000 as your total bankroll for a four-day gambling trip. Next, determine how many gambling sessions you will have each day.

Let's say you decide on two sessions the first day, three the second, three the third, and two the fourth day. That's a total of ten sessions. Divide your total bankroll of $1,000 by this number. The result, $100, is your bankroll for each session. Now physically divide your $1,000 into ten separate $100 "stashes." Keep each session's $100 separate from the others and separate from all the other money you have.

For each session, use only the money that you have set aside; don't dip into other session bankrolls or your other funds, no matter what happens.

The next part of your wager-management plan is to determine how you will bet in each game. Consider first the betting unit. That's the amount you enter a game with—or the minimum bet as posted for that table or machine.

This could be 25¢, $1, $2, $5, or $10, for example. Keep in mind that you cannot leave as a winner by constantly betting the minimum at table games. That's known as flat betting. To be successful at gambling, you must use a progressive betting method.

In other words, after a win you must increase your bet by either one unit or half the amount of your win, whichever you choose. This is known as pressing your bet. After a loss, go back to your original, or minimum, bet. Never press your bet on a loss. (The Martingale system advocates pressing after a loss, but I haven't met one serious gambler who agrees with that.)

You will hear more about progressive betting, and wager management in general, throughout this book. These are keys to your gambling education.

Use them and reap the rewards!

Wager management above all means knowing when to quit . . . when to cut your losses and take a break or find another game.

There are always other games and other machines for the diversified player.

Your "stop-loss"—the point where you will quit a session because you're losing—should be half of the session's bankroll. If you get down to that point and have nothing to show for your effort, it's time to go shopping, see the sights, or take a nap.

Quitting at this halfway point prevents you from losing your total session bankroll, which might tempt you to go into your pocket or, even worse, to pull out your credit card.

When you do that, who is in control? You or the casino?

Let someone else, not you, pay the bills for the casino.

Let's wrap up this discussion with just a few more essential principles of wager management: Settle for small victories. Make a habit of taking stock of your money and counting it frequently. Pay attention. Know what you are doing. Keep control of your money at all times. Put your wager-management plan in writing.

Remember, you have a huge advantage over uneducated gamblers when you make effective decisions about what to bet, which games to play, and when to quit. Knowing when to quit, in particular, takes away the casino's biggest advantage. You are under no obligation to give back your winnings.

Most casinos offer free gaming lessons (for example, for craps, roulette, and blackjack). While you will learn the rules of the games, you will not learn the best strategies. The casinos won't give that information away, but I will!

Take control away from the casino and reclaim it for yourself.

To do that, exercise your Intelligent Gambling Quotient and remember: Not only do you have good luck with education, but also you are making your luck!

Some General Gambling Lingo

3

Sometimes when you listen to people talking in a casino, it seems like they're speaking a foreign language. So, in relation to each of the games discussed, I've provided brief explanations of common gambling lingo.

Before discussing these games individually, however, I've listed some general casino lingo that you're likely to hear around tables or sports books. Knowing some of these terms will impress your playing buddies and will surely add fun to your next casino experience.

Basic Terms

Barber pole: The colorful name used for more than one denomination in a stack of chips.

Cage: The friendly casino cashiers and lots of moolah are located here.

Case bet: A player's bet that contains all remaining chips on the table, or "all in."

Cheques: The correct term for playing chips used at a gaming table.

Coloring up: When you take those five-dollar chips and exchange them for larger denominations, possibly hundred-dollar chips, you are coloring up.

Dime: A bet of $1,000.

Dirty money: The losing bets gathered by the dealer.

Exposure: The maximum number of dollars a sports book stands to lose.

Foreign: Refers to cheques from another casino.

Grind: This term is used for playing it out on a consistent basis at the tables. A player "grinds" out planned bets using knowledgeable probabilities of the game.

Handle: Total amount of money bet.

Hold: Betting monies that are placed in the gaming table slots. The dollar value is generally stated as a percentage.

Nickel: A bet of $500.

Sleeper: A forgotten table bet originally wagered by the player and/or dealer.

Toke: More than a "tip of your hat," this is the gratuity paid to a dealer or casino employee.

Vigorish: The casino's fee or commission paid, during specific wagers in the games of baccarat, craps, and/or sports book.

The Players

Agent: A player who forms a partnership with a dealer with the intention of cheating a particular casino.

Chalkeater: A player who bets only favorites.

Eighty-six, 86: You are outta there, man. Casino rules allow the exclusion and/or eviction of undesirable gamblers.

George: A generous tipper to both table dealers and other casino employees.

Handicapper: Someone who does the research beforehand to make knowledgeable bets. This data includes statistics, news, weather, and injuries.

Mechanic: The term used for a dice or card cheat who utilizes sleight of hand while playing.

Railbird: An observer who hangs around a gaming table. His intention may be to "lift" chips from unsuspecting players.

Rathole: A player who slowly puts away chips during play to give the appearance that he or she is not ahead of the game.

Scamdicapper: A player with outlandish claims about win percentages and game expectations.

Sharp: A pro sports bettor.

Shill: Describes a casino employee who plays the tables to garner business for the casino.

Square: A rookie sports bettor.

Tom: A nontipper.

And More . . .

Comp: As in freebie, any of the dining, beverage, and hotel-room benefits received by casino players based on their wagering and time played.

Cross fire: Not the TV program—the dealers chatting it up about everything else but the live game that is going on in front of them.

Croupier: Pronounced CREW-pee-ay, it is French, mon ami, for the dealer of the gaming table. Mais oui!

Daubing: Utilizing a dab of oil or other substance to "mark" the backs of the cards for easy recognition during the game. This tactic is perfectly aboveboard for those who practice daubing legally.

Eye in the sky: A management monitor who watches the action as the casino staff surveys the floor.

Pips: The spades, clubs, hearts, and diamonds found on a deck of cards. The kings, jacks, and queens sure are pretty, but the lone ace gets the top prize, don't you agree?

Sawdust joint: Name used for a not so elegant casino offering low table and slot betting minimums. Yes, it's a dump, but you can play cheap!

Now let the games begin . . .

The Ten Best
Bets in the Casino

4

Enter the casino showroom and take a good look at your surroundings. You will see lights, action, people coming and going, no clocks, free drinks, plus lots of slots and gaming tables. It's all designed to lure you inside, get you playing, and keep you playing. (Sometimes I think they pump extra oxygen into the air to keep the players playing. How often have you received a second, third, or fourth wind while gambling and felt like you could play for hours without getting tired?)

Of course, the biggest lure of all in a casino are the chips. These red, white, green, and black pieces look like "funny money." They may tempt you to think that you are playing an innocent game, such as Monopoly. However, those chips represent real money—your hard-earned money.

Respect them just as you would respect a real $1, $5, $10, or $20 bill.

When you walk into a casino, your plan is to observe and shop for value. It's like buying a car. You don't buy the first car you see; you shop around.

After you look around, test-drive a few of the games. Then you can make the best, most profitable deal with your hard-earned money. As a gambler with a high Intelligent Gambling Quotient, you will know that a casino has ten "models" that are good bets.

These ten best games are those where the casino's edge is below 3 percent when the player follows correct basic strategy.

Your goal is to always try to keep the casino edge under 3 percent.

Percentages play a big part in our choice of casino games, and will be discussed in detail as we proceed from table to table.

We also will cover correct strategies and skills for each of the ten selected "superior" games, to which the next ten chapters will be devoted.

Secrets of
Successful Slot Play

5

L urid Luck, Crazy Clunking, Sensual Greed, Hypnotic Fascination,
Ultimate Urge . . . yes, we are still talking about gambling! These are
some of the nicknames for slot machines, which, to return to our automobile analogy, are the most popular "model" on the showroom floor.

The most important factor in winning at slots is playing the right
machine, and there is much more to this than is generally known.

The best slots—those that return the highest percentage—are in Las
Vegas, where competition is fiercest for the gambler's dollar. In Vegas, I advise that you get off the Strip and go where the locals play. The locals don't
play on the Strip with the tourists. They prefer the downtown or "outer
loop" casinos, which offer better payoffs to cater to these local residents.

As an educated player, you have just as much right as the locals to take
advantage of these better payoffs.

Above all, when choosing slot machines, avoid the tight (low-paying) slots in restaurants, bars, airports, and supermarkets. These are set
up for people on the go to put their change in. Don't be one of them!

Wherever you play slots, though, you should know the basics about
the machines. The outside of a slot machine has standard features, but few
people bother to know what goes on inside. That's where the computerized random number generator, or RNG, resides.

RNG: Random Number Generator

Every slot machine contains an RNG, a computer program that generates random number sequences related to a reel result that is then duplicated. Higher payouts are assigned fewer numbers, while lower payouts are assigned more numbers. The RNG then sequences through a series of numbers, determining a result when the player triggers the spin button or slot handle. This program is also designed to determine the slot's average payout percentage.

The RNG program works even when the machine is idle.

So if no one is playing when the RNG selects a winning combination—let's say at 5:26 A.M. on October 6—then that winning combination passes without notice. Your timing has to be correct down to the last millisecond to catch the machine when its RNG comes up with a winner. In addition, the RNG does not remember what it has done in the past. So it could pay off two or three times in a row. Therefore, after any jackpot win, try three more pulls. If you get nothing in return, move on and congratulate yourself on the big win.

You have to search for the slot of your dreams, because most models give a low return on your investment. Before entering any casino, check outside for signs advertising slots with at least a 98 percent payback. Those are the better, looser slots.

However, don't expect the casino to have only 98-percenters. Check the fine print on those signs proclaiming "the loosest slots in town." You will notice that the key words are "up to 98 percent payback." Most of any casino's slots do not pay back that much. Once inside, you can begin shopping to find the best-paying slots in the house. Look for "signature slots" with the casino's name on them or a sign saying, "guaranteed slots."

These are specially designed, generally looser slots.

Larger casinos are offering "certified" slots, guaranteed to payback 100 percent. Usually dollar slots, these are an excellent bet if all of the machines do in fact return 100 percent.

Casinos have to tell you—by law in most states—if all of the certified machines in that carousel are set at the advertised rate, or if the advertised rate is simply an average of all the machines in that carousel. When in doubt, ask. And keep asking until you get an authoritative answer.

As I guide you on this shopping trip, we'll look at the terms "loose" and "tight" in relation to slots.

Slot machines in Nevada generally have paybacks between 92 and 98.5 percent. Nevada law prohibits return levels below 75 percent.

Slots with higher payout probabilities (percentage rates) are called "loose."

"Tight" slots, on the other hand, have lower payout probabilities (percentage rates).

A machine will pay a couple of coins on a certain symbol combination, such as two or three cherries. If these same cherries replace another symbol that doesn't pay, presto—you have a loose machine. In a tight slot, the reverse is true. In other words, the more paying symbols a slot machine has, the greater the probability of payouts.

Some of the loosest slots—even so-called 98-plus-percenters—still average only an 80 percent payback to the players. That's because players don't play the maximum number of coins. Slots make up to 70 percent of a casino's revenues. Let's stop giving the casinos what we players can rightfully claim!

Now back to our search for the best slots—and ways to avoid the tight ones. There are three types of slots:

1. Basic slots, with a single payline and a constant jackpot.
2. Progressives, which offer a changing, ever-growing jackpot.
3. Bonus video multiline slots—the latest gaming trend.

This chapter discusses all three types.

Basic Slots

Basic, or "flat-top," slots have a constant top jackpot that does not change, no matter how much the machine is played. They usually have an unchanging payback percentage rate. Basic slots tend to give smaller wins to keep you in business and extend your playing time.

The payline for basic slots is the single stripe on the window where you see the reels spinning and stopping. You win or lose depending on what symbols stop directly on this stripe.

Examples of basic slot machines that have higher paybacks are Diamond-type slots, such as Double or Triple Diamonds—a two- or three-coin-maximum slot with a single payline that can double or triple your win for a particular three-reel combination.

Other good slot bets are the Red, White, and Blue 7's and Blazing 7's. They all have single-play payoff lines with two- or three-coin maximums.

Choose basic slots that have the fewest reels. The odds of winning with a three-reel machine are greater than the odds of winning with a five-reel slot.

As you look for loose slots, think not only in terms of slot type but also about what the casinos call "slot mix" or placement. For example, if I am a casino manager, I want to place my slots in whatever way will best attract the most players. So, for instance, I'll put my loose slots in high-traffic areas where a passerby can see a lot of slot players winning often. That will encourage the passerby to stop and play the slots, too, because people are motivated by what they see happening around them. I also want slot players held captive deep in the underbelly of the casino, where they will get comfortable and relaxed . . . and therefore play more and longer.

You'll often see slot players spinning their reels near the entertainment lounge or in public places, such as around the gaming tables or the casino entrance. As a casino manager, I know these people are going to be there for a short time only, and then they'll move on. So don't expect to find loose slots in these locations. For these reasons, you should never pick a slot machine at random. Instead, analyze a slot's location and decide if it's likely to be a spot for a loose machine.

In other words, crack the slot-mix code. To do just that, check out slots in these spots:

1. In crosswalks—where players cross to get from one group of machines to another.
2. Where slots are located on both sides of an aisle, in areas leading to and from the cashier or change booths.
3. Any elevated bank of slots. ·

20

4.   Near the coffee shop. (These are often loose so that gamblers taking a coffee break will see all the action and be eager to hurry back to the floor.)

A lot of basic slot players like to play two machines at a time, side by side. If I were a casino manager, I would take advantage of this and place tight slots next to loose ones. What one giveth, the other taketh away. Therefore never play two slots next to each other.

And, for the same reason, don't play next to a winning machine.

When a player next to me wins, I congratulate him or her and move on to another slot.

At one of my seminars, a student exclaimed that he and his wife usually sat side by side when playing slots, so they could share the winnings. When I explained why this was not a good idea, he said, "Now I'll have to tell my wife to get lost."

Everyone in the room smiled as his wife gave him the elbow poke.

As you look for the best slots, spread yourself around. It takes a little time to find them, but that's part of the fun.

After you think you have located a loose machine, read all the posted information before you play. Take your time; there is no need to hurry. After all, if you're gambling for two or three days, shouldn't you be on a mini-vacation, getting a little rest and relaxation? So enjoy your surroundings and relax.

What's the rush?

Don't rush while you play, either. Take your time so you can make sure you have received all the money due you when you win.

The locals know that they have to write down a winning slot's number—not just the slot's location in the casino. That's because any machine can be moved at any time at the whim of the casino manager's slot-placement strategy.

Writing supplies are necessary for another reason: to keep track of your wins and losses. Any jackpot over $1,200 must be reported to the IRS. To lower your tax burden, in some states you can offset your wins by your losses, although you can't claim a net loss. Record keeping is essential in case you hit it big.

Another way to find the best slots is to talk with other slot players.

21

An "us against the casino" mentality makes most people willing to share information. This is a two-way street; make sure you give as much information as you receive.

Always know how much money you have at any given time, thus practicing sound wager management. Remember, too, that one of the principles of wager management is knowing when to quit. Never, never stay too long at a machine. Believe me, there is nothing worse than a slotaholic hangover. The casino advantage kicks in when you overstay your welcome.

After five pulls with no return, get out of there. Be a hit-and-run winner.

If you are tempted to stay at a machine, keep this in mind: Most jackpot wins happen in the first five to ten minutes of play with a small cash outlay. So if a slot doesn't produce for you in fairly short order, get upward and onward, looking for another slot.

Here are three examples of what I call a "short win." These jackpot stories were previously published in *Casino Players Ezine*.

Diamonds Are a Girl's Best Friend

The Marilyn Monroe Diamond Cinema slot is a favorite of Karen Smith's, and after only fifteen minutes and $40 worth of play she was rewarded with a "shimmering" jackpot of $2,155,280.

Karen, of Cherokee Village, Arkansas, likes to play at Imperial Palace hotel casino in Biloxi, Mississippi. She didn't realize she won until she checked the meter again. "I was in disbelief. I needed confirmation from my friend Lois. I am going to share my winning by helping others," said Smith.

Travelin' in Riches and Safety

Debra A. Pannelli of Cape May Court House chose to play a *Jeopardy!* quarter progressive slot at Bally's, Atlantic City, which led to the "riches" part of her story. Pannelli, a housewife and new grandmother, started playing at Bally's last year and had visited five times before she "struck bigtime gold" with a $1,703,134 jackpot. Debra and her husband decided to

22

travel from one end of the casino floor to the other and, after an invest-ment of only $20, the clamor of bells and spinning lights announced their big win. After calling her mother and her son, Debra said one of the first things she would do with her winnings is purchase a truck with an ex-tended cab so her grandson can ride safely around town with her.

New Slot Hits Big

Kathryn Harris's day was off to a rousing start with two jackpot wins of over $3,000 and her husband's take of $2,000 while playing at Boulder Station Casino in Vegas.

Moreover, the hits just kept on coming, with a huge strike of $1.6 million at the new nickel version of the Wheel of Fortune Special Edition video slot. "The game was brandnew and looked like fun, so I played it," Harris said. With less than $20 and a few minutes of her time, the five reels aligned in just the right position.

"Because the game is so new, no one knew what I won. The slot at-tendant had to go find someone to tell us that it was the big one."

This big winner, a Los Angeles bank employee, had made a family trek to Vegas in celebration of Mother's Day for her ninety-year-old mother.

"My mom can't believe that she has lived long enough to see her daughter become a millionaire," Harris said. "And I can't believe it ei-ther!"

Many players ask me if there is a best time of the day or the week to play slots.

Yes, there is. The best time of the day is in the wee hours of the morning (2 to 6 A.M.).

The best days of the week are after a weekend.

In both cases, the crowds are gone during these times, which is part of the strategy.

You will have the big advantage of slot selection—a field of slots awaiting your choice.

In addition, you have a plan: Five spins for a quick hit. Go for it!

However, even if a slot rewards you with some small wins right away, it's not necessarily the best machine you could be playing. That's why you should always test a slot machine before you commit yourself to continued play. Testing applies to straight, basic slot machines, not to progressives, where your aim is to hit the top jackpot with less concern for smaller wins along the way.

Here is a method for testing basic quarter slots:

1. With a buy-in of $10—forty quarters—in hand, play through all $10 and leave all your winnings in the tray or allow the credits to accumulate. Do not combine your wins with any other money, because that would ruin the test.

2. As you play your $10, you may decide to jump ship early for any reason —including hitting the jackpot. If you continue to play until you have played all $10, stop and count your winnings.

3. If your final total is less than 65 percent of your test amount ($6.50 or less in this example), get up and find yourself another slot machine. If your winnings total at least 65 percent, the slot may be in or near an up cycle. Try three more coins and, based on any payouts from that, decide if you want to stay. Of course, if you get back more than your original $10, you have found a sizzling slot! As you continue to play the machine, stash half your winnings. This is now your money—not the casino's! Now, you may say that getting back 65 percent is not so hot. Keep in mind that no slot machine will pay back its preset payoff percentage rate every time. If a casino advertises specific slots as 98 percent return, this will never mean that for each $1 you put in, you will get back 98 cents.

    A lot of first-time players make this mistake.

    What this really means is that over the fiscal long-term cycle of that particular slot machine, it will average payoffs equal to 98 percent of all monies put through it. A long-term cycle can be weeks or even months. In the meantime, a slot with an average 98 percent payoff rate will sometimes pay off at 130 percent and sometimes at 50 percent . . . sometimes at 28 percent and sometimes at 502 percent. When the machine is paying off at the lower percentages, it's in a down cycle. When it's paying off at the higher percentages, it's in an up cycle.

Of course, all good things must end, and you know that even a sizzling slot in an up cycle will eventually have a down cycle. The informed gambler knows the signs of an impending down cycle.

One sign is that the machine just hit the top jackpot. Any wins after that are more likely to be small wins that are not worth prolonged play.

Another sign is when the machine starts hitting a lot of near misses—symbol combinations that are almost winners but not quite.

It's a funny thing, but in both these cases, you may be tempted to keep playing.

In the first situation, you are tempted to continue because you just won, and you might think, remembering the RNG process, that the machine has another win in it just waiting for you. In the second scenario, all those "almost wins" seem to be saying, "Next time . . . next time." In both cases, you should resist the temptation.

Additionally, slot players should look for two-coin-maximum non-progressive machines. Whereas a two-coin machine may pay 80 coins for three double bars with two coins in, a three-coin machine may pay 120 coins for the same combination.

But remember, you had to gamble an extra coin. With each spin, therefore, the payouts are generally equal. Three-coin machines only look more lucrative in their payoff structure. Players who play the three-coin machines will spend considerably more than players who invest more of their playing time and money in the preferred two-coin machines, which gets them more pulls on that slot and more chances to win a jackpot. Unless the machine is progressive (we will discuss these later), stay away from three-coin slots.

You will want to seek out those slots that pay double jackpots on certain payline combinations. The principle of this "double" symbol is very simple—whenever it appears on the payline in combination with any other symbols that normally would have made a winning combination, the payoff amount is doubled. These double symbols also substitute for any other pay symbol.

Look closely to see which machine you are playing. Not all machines will double or quadruple all payouts or have double-jackpot win possibilities. When choosing a "double" machine, it is important not to confuse the symbol with wild cherries or any other symbols noted on the machines' payoff display as being wild. Wild symbols merely sub for any other paying symbol, but do not double the payoff.

Machines that have only two of these double-jackpot symbols (one on the first reel and one on the second reel) usually pay the top jackpot by combining both of the double symbols in conjunction with a 7 on the third reel (Red, White, and Blue 7's). These machines are just as good to play as those employing the three double symbols, providing it is a two-coin-maximum single-payline machine. It makes sense that any basic slot with a 1,000-coin top payout will hit more often than RWBs with 5,000- or 10,000-coin top jackpots.

Blackjack players will argue loud and long with me for this, but there are researchers who theorize that you can make just as much money on an hourly basis playing slots as playing Black Jack.

Cost per hour to play slots:

Denomination	2 coins	3 coins
Nickel	$60.00	$90.00
Quarter	$300.00	$450.00
Dollar	$1200.00	$1800.00

I rest my case for playing two-coin machines. With quarter machines (the most popular slots), I would have an extra $150 to play with and 300 extra spins or pulls at two-coin machines.

You will almost never find these basic two-coin slots together in the same carousel. Carousel slots are usually mixes of good and bad machines. The thinking is that people will be attracted to a carousel if they see one player cleaning up.

Progressive Slots

Once upon a time, there were lottery tickets to build dreams on. Then IGT, a slot manufacturer, with the loud approval of its casino clients, introduced the first progressive slot in March 1986.

This network of slots was connected locally, then expanded to participating gaming states, nationwide; now there is an international link that reaches into Canada, Europe, and Asia. IGT, always the vanguard in slot-sland, was followed by Bally's Thrillion series and Aristocrat's Hyperlink systems. The many versions of progressive slots from these three manufacturers include familiar names like Megabucks, Jeopardy!, Wheel of Fortune, Quarter Million$, and Cash Express.

There are many more progressives to choose from today as slot manufacturers pair their progressive versions with a bonus slot release—for example, Addams Family or Jeopardy! These versions are leased by the participating casinos, which receive a small percentage, while the manufacturers maintain the equipment and pay out the "millionaire-producing" jackpots.

Some casinos install exclusive or proprietary slot progressives.

The big name at land-based casinos is Megabucks, linked to casinos nationwide. You must play $3 to be eligible to win the millions. Because this and other progressives usually don't give as many smaller wins as straight slots do, my usual "five losses and you're outta there" rule does not necessarily apply. Try 10 pulls—for $30—on these slots and see what happens.

The largest slot machine jackpot to date at a land-based casino was $39,713,982, won won on Friday, March 21, 2003, on an IGT Megabucks machine at the Excalibur in Las Vegas. The winner, who requested anonymity, was a twenty-five-year-old software engineer from Los Angeles. He said he had played about $100 on the machine when he turned his head away from it for an instant.

When he looked at the machine again, the winning symbols had lined up. Since the beginning, more than 250 millionaires have emerged thanks to IGT slots.

How do these ever-increasing jackpots grow? Well, approximately 10 percent of every dollar fed into the progressive slot goes directly to the primary jackpots, awaiting the "magic winning touch." Because of this feature, progressive overall payback percentages will not be as high as those or basic slots, with their constant jackpot amount; 80 percent is not uncommon, and the jackpot may be paid out over twenty years, instead of all at once. Most players are not aware that there are two levels of progressive jackpots: primary and secondary.

A primary jackpot is the top prize award, achieved by the specific combination hit. In the case of Megabucks, these are the Megabuck symbols, which, lined up correctly, produce a bountiful payday. This top jackpot is usually displayed with the biggest sign and numbers above the carousel or bank of machines.

Secondary jackpots are displayed on smaller screens mounted below the big screen of the primary jackpot. These are hit more frequently and therefore will not pay out as large a sum of money.

Before playing any single group of progressives, check out the primary and secondary jackpots, and then compare other surrounding progressives to see how high those jackpots are relative to their starting amounts. Additionally, progressives online offer an attractive option for playing these massive-jackpot slots. Several sites track progressive totals as they grow, so you can best determine the ideal bet. After a progressive jackpot is hit, the meter automatically resets to the base jackpot amount.

In the future, I believe, million-dollar progressive jackpots will become the norm, and will be paid as instant winners instead of being paid out over a twenty-year period. Penny slots now offer up to $1 million jackpots with the maximum number of coins in play.

Online high-dollar progressives are here and can only multiply, to the delight of all slots players. Very soon, everyone will be able to make that "golden spin." Have fun with this special line of slots. Be sure to bet the maximum number of coins every time, and in the end may all your progressive wins be progressively profitable.

Bonus Slots

The current gaming trend of bonus slots has become the most fun, graphically loaded, and glitziest of the slots. I think how I laughed at my video arcade friends back then—but guess who's playing these arcade party machines now?

Bonus slots are known as "branded machines," "brand recognition" or "participation" games, or "interactive" or "banking" slots. Regular slot players will recognize the names: Monopoly, Elvis, Let's Make a Deal, Jeopardy!, Yahtzee, Piggy Bankin', and Reel 'Em In.

One of the first versions on the scene was Piggy Bankin', where the progressive jackpot grows until the "break the bank" symbol stops on the last reel.

The main goal of these games is to play the reels to win a second-chance bonus round, where the real money is.

Since the bonus slots trend (which includes reel and video versions) first exploded in 2000, I have published over five hundred bonus slot reviews. Here are three previously published in *Casino Players Ezine*:

50 Lions

This is the first fifty-payline slot introduced into the slots playground. The innovative concepts of this slot are more than two thousand possible winning combinations for every spin, more symbols, and two additional rows of symbols.

Each credit buys two paylines for this "kingly" jungle-themed slot, and only two, rather than three, same neighboring symbols will pay.

Here are a couple of features from the long menu of winning combinations for this slot.

- Three flower scatter-pay symbols trigger ten free games, while a wild diamond symbol is added to each of the second through fifth reels.
- The wild symbol subs for all other symbols here.
- If the three flower symbols appear during a free spin, another five free games are added to the free spin round, equaling fifteen spins.
- Last, and certainly not least, the King's Jackpot is one million pennies—a very regal $10,000.

Hollywood Squares: Premier Night

Continuing with the success of this popular game show series, this one boasts a top box display of a grand limo and searchlights shining on bonus numbers. One of the bonus rounds occurs when three or more searchlight symbols land on an active payline on the righthand reels, prompting the Searchlight Bonus. Searchlights at the top box light up the credit spots, eventually stopping on a value up to five hundred coins. However, if two searchlights shine on a credit amount and a Double Pay, the reward is doubled. If the bonus spot is lit up or you line up three limo symbols, then it's on to the Premier Night Bonus.

The set of TV's *Hollywood Squares*, a giant tic-tac-toe board, appears and Joan Rivers, via video, directs you to pick one of the limo doors or the sunroof, revealing the game's nine celebrities. The player receives five picks to win a tic-tac-toe. If one of the celebrities goes to the Secret Square, there is the possibility of more games. If a Super Tic-Tac-Toe is won, you are prompted to pick one of five boxes for an additional reward of up to 1,000 credits.

The scatter pay for this version is for three or more champagne symbols, paying up to 200 credits, depending on your selection. The spotlight is on you to step right up and play the "game of the stars."

I Love Lucy: Chocolate Factory

Locate that familiar heart logo from the classic series. When you hear bits of the memorable dialogue from the show, you have arrived. Our lovable Lucy demands, "So whaddya wanna bet?" Fred and Ethel become visible when you touch the screen, along with other icons, such as Lucy's hat and Ricky's conga drum and panama hat.

Line up five heart-shaped logos for the top bonus award and hear Desi sing the theme song. The classic bonus, triggered when you line up three or more of the same symbols, begins with a presentation of several still frames for your selection. After an entertaining look-see, your bonus amount appears. Scatter pays are awarded for three Club Babaluo symbols.

Let's not forget the reason for this game, for when three Lucy's Chocolate Factory icons appear, the player gets to select eight chocolates directly from the assembly line, with bonus amounts attached. The most fun for me is tapping the button rapidly. This brings out the supervisor, who yells, "Speed it up," while my credits mount quickly.

When you approach a bonus slot you will immediately see many more graphics than at a basic slot or a progressive; twenty-five symbols or more will fill up the screen in front of you. The buttons in front of you will offer five, nine or up to fifty paylines.

Many versions come in penny denominations, but with maximums of up to 225 coins for pennies and 45 coins for nickels. That's $2.25 per spin, folks. The RNG remains very active when the machine is idle, and the number of possibilities with graphic-rich bonus slots is staggering. Payouts are much more frequent, usually every two to three spins.

As always, read all the information posted. There many more pay-out options with these versions, so it's crucial to review the help menu that explains the game rules and the paylines crisscrossing the screen grid. Scatter-pay wild symbols are paid when appearing anywhere on the screen. Bonus-round top points should factor in how you select bonus types or versions. Bonus secondary jackpots can produce up to 10,000 coins and primary or top jackpots of 100,000 or more, as printed on the machine. I learn a lot simply by observing seated players; it's a good idea to watch the bonus round in action before a final decision.

Warning: Casinos set up bonus versions simply because they know players will get carried away with accumulating credits and a chance at the bonus round. As with any other casino game, wager management and discipline are essential. Be an intelligent gambler. This is critical with bonus machines, because higher betting amounts dictate that a bill acceptor is used. Be sure to keep track of monies gobbled up by the bill acceptor.

Once you begin to play, be sure to activate all paylines but one or two coins per line, rather than the top forty-five- or ninety-nickel maximum, at $2.25 and $4.50 per spin.

As you can see, bonus slots are played differently from basic slots, where my usual advice of playing five-coins-maximum coin spins is "out the window."

Bonus slots are "reel" enjoyment and, with correct strategy, can be particularly profitable.

There are many misconceptions about slot machines, which this introduction should begin to dispel. In case it hasn't, here are the ten most common misconceptions about the game. For each, I've added a factual refutation:

Misconception No. 1: Someone hits a jackpot at the machine you were just playing; that could have been your jackpot!

This is not true, because of the random number generator (RNG) in the slot machine. It's constantly in motion, picking different number combinations. Even when the machine is idle, the RNG continues shuffling, faster than you can pull the handle or press that spin button. To win, you have to be in exactly the right place at exactly the right time. That takes luck, the nature of the beast with slots.

So don't beat yourself up if someone comes along right after you and hits a jackpot. And don't be afraid to leave a slot machine because you think this might happen to you. Think about this instead: Do blackjack players worry about who is going to sit in their seat after they leave the table? Of course not.

So when you're ready to find another slot, go ahead. Move on.

Misconception No.2: The casinos can "flip a switch" to make machines tight or loose.

Nope.

Only the slot manufacturer can make any changes to a slot machine. In addition, the Gaming Control Board does not allow casinos to make changes.

Misconception No. 3: Hot coins mean the machine will win, and cold coins mean the machine will lose.

The only reason a machine delivers hot coins is because of the lights near the hopper.

Misconception No. 4: If an attendant or mechanic opens your machine, it will stop paying.

Usually, an attendant opens a machine only to correct a problem or to refill the hopper with coins. Don't worry; the RNG continues to work when the reset button is pushed to restart play. Sometimes a slot mechanic will give a player two or three free pulls—especially if the player is polite.

However, if stopping for a mechanic makes you lose your rhythm, you have two choices: When the mechanic is done, play another three pulls and decide whether to stay or leave; or leave when your play is interrupted.

Misconception No. 5: Higher-denomination slots have more payouts.

While $5 and over slots naturally have higher payouts, they are not the only slots you should play for higher payouts. Certainly, the casinos do not want to discourage the dollar, fifty-cent or quarter players. Quarter machines account for 25 percent of total slots revenue, and you just know casinos won't fool with that bottom line by offering better payouts only for high-end slots. On the other hand, basic nickel slots do have lower payouts because the maintenance costs are higher. They are played regularly and require more attention than other slots. Multiline nickel bonus slots are the exception here.

Misconception No. 6: Players should play less than the maximum number of coins until the machine starts to pay.

This myth really scares me, because it goes against basic slot-playing strategy and could be very costly to the player.

Remember, the RNG doesn't know if you're putting in one coin or three. You gain no advantage by trying to pump or prime that slot machine for the jackpot, because you have no idea when that jackpot will be. The next symbol combination to come your way has already been determined before you hit that spin button. Trust me on this: If you can't afford to play the maximum number of coins, drop down to a lower-priced machine.

Misconception No. 7: Players should move up to higher denomination machines in hopes of better payoffs.

This is the reverse of Misconception No. 6 and can be very costly, too, because you will lose more money at a faster rate.

Misconception No. 8: You've put so much money into a machine, it must be ready to hit. You deserve to win!

Yes, you do deserve to win, but the length of time a slot is played without winning has no bearing on its readiness to pay. Any slot can go months or years without paying its top jackpot. It maintains its programmed pay-off percentage rate by paying smaller wins.

Misconception No. 9: Machines don't pay if you use a casino slot club card.

Tell that to the RNG! It doesn't know what a slot card is, and it certainly doesn't care if you use one.

Misconception No. 10: Play the machines nearest the doors or aisles.

While you may be more comfortable in these seats, we know where the best slots are, based on slot mix.

Enough said.

Review: A Slots Quiz

Okay, class, it's test time.

I've created this test for novice and veteran slot players. I find that slot players possess different levels of expertise and education.

There's the group that believes that all you have to know is how to push a spin button or pull that handle. Some think all slots are alike and pay the same. Others have not updated themselves on slot machines and are bewildered by the versions arriving frequently on the casino floor. We all need to upgrade our slots education to stay current, myself included.

I visit casinos at least once a week to research new versions and test strategies.

Tough work that must be done!

I offer this quiz in the hopes of helping you sooner to hear the sound of "raining coins."

Let's get started . . .

1) What is an RNG?
   A Really Nice Gambling
   B Random Number Generator
   C Right Number Gaming

2) What are the three types of slots?
   A Basic, progressive, and bonus slots
   B Red, White, and Blue 7's
   C Flat-tops, Megabucks, and Double Diamonds

3) Are the higher-denomination-slot payouts better?
   A Yes
   B No
   C All the same

4) What are loose and tight machines?
   A Loose machines have more graphic symbols, tight have fewer
   B Loose machines have better payouts, tight machines less
   C Loose machines offer more slot versions, tight machines fewer choices

5) What is a slot-mix?
   A Slots are placed back to back on either side of aisle?
   B All the high denomination slots are in one area of the casino?
   C Casino management's placement of loose or tight slots?

6) What is a hold percentage?
   A Monies held by winning slot players
   B The percentage of coins held by the casino
   C The percentage of coins through the slots

7) Do some slots have a higher "hit" frequency?
   A Yes
   B No
   C All the same

8) What is a multiplier slot?
   A A slot that has multiple graphics and symbols
   B One that pays more for more coins played on certain winning combinations
   C One that multiplies your win no matter how many coins played

9) What is a nudge slot?
   A When the wild symbol combination pays
   B When a certain combination nudges you to the bonus round
   C A paying symbol dropping up or down on the center payline for a win

10) What's a hit-and-run winner?
    A A slot player who plays the new Baseball Bonus Slot
    B A slot player who uses a token slug and grabs the payout
    C A slot player who plays five-coin maximums testing for payouts

11) What's a short win?
    A A small jackpot
    B A win just before you run out of money
    C A large win with a small cash outlay

12) What is "flying solo"?
    A Gambling alone
    B Slot players who play one coin only
    C The only winner of a progressive jackpot

13) What is a "certified" slot?
    A A slot with a certificate from the manufacturer
    B A slot that is guaranteed to pay back a large percentage, as high as 98 percent or more
    C A slot that is certified to have a certain number of symbols

14) Do all "certified" slots in the carousel or bank offer high payouts?
    A Yes
    B No
    C Yes and No, depending on the casino

15) Will all "certified" slots pay out their advertised rate all the time?
    A Yes
    B No
    C Can I sell you some land in Pago Pago?

16) Which is more lucrative, pulling the handle or pressing the spin button on slots?
   A Handle
   B Spin button
   C Neither; they're both the same

17) What is a wild-pay slot?
   A A slot that has more wild symbols than 7's
   B A slot that offers double, triple, and more with wild symbols
   C When only wild party animals are paid jackpots

18) How many games per hour does the average slot player play?
   A 500 games per hour
   B 600 games per hour
   C 700 games per hour

19) Are there higher dollar values for some progressives in the casino?
   A Yes
   B No
   C They're all the same

20) Easy point: What's "Call Attendant"?
   A A large hand-paid cash jackpot
   B A machine is broken and needs maintenance
   C My slot-club card points have reached their limit

Answers

1) B. Random Number Generator: a computer chip placed inside each slot that is programmed to generate multiple combinations of symbols and payouts. A selection is picked randomly, thus determining the final outcome. A busy little drone.

2) A. The three types of slots are basic, (a.k.a straight slots or "flat-tops"), which have a constant jackpot; progressives, with an ever-increasing jackpot (the latest gaming trend); and bonus video slots, which offer a bonus round for extra winnings. Although the RNG runs all three types, there are different playing strategies for each type.

3) A. Yes, higher denominations ($5 and up) have a higher hit frequency; however, it is relative when you are investing more of your gambling bankroll. Start off with quarter machines, which account for 25 percent of total slot revenue and are the most popular slots.

Streeetch those gambling bucks.

4) B. Loose machines are a slot player's dream. They are programmed with more paying symbols and combinations, resulting in better payouts. Tight machines are the opposite. Yikes, they're stingy.

5) C. The slot mix is known as slot placement. Casino management places different slot versions, a combination of loose and tight machines, on the casino floor. Loose slots are found in high-traffic areas that can be seen by "wannabe slot winners" from many angles in the casino.

6) B. The percentage of coins played that the casinos keep in their hot little hands. The looser 98 percent slots hold $2 while returning $98 to the player.

But hold on: That percentage is over the long term—perhaps months—while short-term return percentages can bounce around more than a roulette ball.

7) A. With bonus video slots, hit frequencies have been increased to a high of every two to three spins. While you don't always get your original bet back, these graphically rich slots provide the most entertainment for your money. Wager management is the key here. It's not always wise to bet the maximum number of coins every time, and a higher hit frequency doth not necessarily a winning slot make.

8) B. Stated simply, the more coins played, the better the winning payouts. Particular symbol payouts, as per the slot schedule, are multiplied by the number of coins played. This can mean the difference between a two-coin payout and a ten-coin payout.

So one bar, two bars, three bars—oh yeah!

9) C. Come on, baby, drop that paying symbol down and give Mama a big win.

It could be a basketball, a diamond, a cherry, or a wild symbol. You just need a little nudge up or down to that center payline and you are in the money.

10) C. Slot players who "test" a slot before continued play by spinning the reels five times with the maximum number of coins in play each time. If

there are no payouts during that period, you are outta there. By the way, I suggest you not try B—the casinos don't like it.

11) C. This happens all the time. A large jackpot is hit with a minimal cash outlay. Fifteen bucks gets you thousands. Now, that's a long win on a short chance. Take the money and run!

12) B. Slot players who play only one coin; I call them "onesies." I know I advocate wager management, but this is wager suicide. I suggest that you drop down a denomination and play the maximum number of coins so at least you are in the running for the top jackpot without the "slot bends" of missing out because you should have played just one more coin. The only exception here comes with the bonus multiline slots.

13) B. Most casinos promote their "certified" slots at a bank or carousel with large flashing, neon lights, generally near the entrance to the casino. Like carnival barkers, these round neon lights seem to yell, "Step right up, folks, see the slots with huge payouts, play the big winners, yowser, yowser, yowser." Most certified slots are at least dollar denominations.

14) C. A casino can legitimately advertise a very high payback even if only one of the machines has the advertised payback—sneaky, right? However, the casino must tell you whether the payback is for all or just one of the machines. Ask the slot manager if all of the slots are certified. If the answer is no, run, don't walk, to another casino. If only one or two are certified, you could spend a lot of money looking for that "slot in the haystack."

15) B. Certified slots payouts, whether they are advertised at 98 percent or 100 percent, are programmed over an average period of time that could be weeks or months. As you know, timing is crucial in the slots game and the same goes for the certified versions.

Don't stay too long.

Determine the total amount you want to wager before you play, and then have fun streeetching your gambling bankroll.

16) C. There is no difference, fellow slot players. Manufacturers still add on the handles as a holdover from the Bronze-Age days of slots. The day is coming when the handle will be eliminated and we will surely yearn for the good ol' days.

17) B. The wild symbol substitutes for a win, double wild symbols multiplies a win, and generally three wild symbols nets you the top jackpot on the payline. There are many more wild slots out there now. However,

keep this in mind before selecting one. The higher the payout multipliers (five times, ten times, and so on), the lower the probability of a payout. Therefore, seek out the double and triple wild slots.

18) A. 500 games per hour on average. These stats can change, depending upon whether coins are manually inserted or credits are used. There really is no need to hurry, unless you are playing in a slot tournament, and then accelerate to warp speed for the win.

19) A. Oh yeah. Most casinos, including online sites, have a selection of banks or carousels that consist of progressive slots with different primary jackpots. All savvy slot players will want to scout out these slots and play "large."

20) A. It's party time! Big-time payday, with hundreds peeled off into your sweaty, winning palms. All casino players should get this one right and truly enjoy the experience.

<u>Ratings</u>

20–15: Congrats. A veteran player with a slots education degree. Bravo.
14–10: A slots education should be in your future.
9 or less: Psst, over here. All is not lost. I can help.

Even with all this good advice about slots, there is no certainty in gambling except uncertainty. I include slot information in my books because the game is so popular and draws so many players. However, the educated gambler diversifies. If you learn and play only one other game, make it video poker.

We will show you how . . . coming up next.

Top-Paying
Video Poker Play

6

The video poker slot model may take a little practice for novices who are used to automatic-pilot slot machines, but it's easy to learn. If you already know how to play, some points in strategy will make your performance even better.

For beginners, poker hand standings are as follows, from the highest-paying wins to the lowest:

That beautiful royal flush!
Straight flush (consecutive order, all same suit)
Four of a kind
Full house (three of a kind and a pair)
Flush (all same suit, no consecutive order)
Straight (consecutive order, not all same suit)
Three of a kind
Two pair
One pair of jacks or better

A pair of 10s or lower has no value with the majority of video poker versions.

Two things are mandatory if you want to become an educated and prepared video poker player: 1) learning how to read a pay schedule and 2) knowing strategies for all the video poker types and games.

All video poker (VP) payoffs are listed on the payout schedule at each machine. The schedule shows how much you will win when you hit a certain hand with a single coin or any number of coins up to the maximum, which offers the largest payoff. Educated gamblers use this schedule because, unlike slots, the best-paying video poker machines are labeled. That makes your search much easier.

To find out how much a VP machine pays, locate the one-coin payout schedule list, on the far left side of a Jacks or Better version. Scan down to the full house and flush. How many coins are paid for each? We are very interested in a machine that pays nine coins for a full house and six coins for a flush. This is called a 9/6, or "full-pay," machine, and it has a 99.6 percent payback. The percentage of return here, as always, is based on the player using solid basic strategy, such as that provided below.

Video Poker Strategy Cards
Jacks or Better 9/6 Basic VP

DRAW TO THE HAND HIGHER ON THE LIST.
HIGH CARD IS A JACK OR BETTER.

<u>Your hand</u>	<u>No. Cards to Draw</u>
Royal flush	0
Straight flush (SF)	0
4 of a kind	0
Four-card royal	1
Full house	0
four-card straight flush	1
Flush	0
3 of a kind	2
Straight	0
2 pair	1
High pair	3
Three-card royal flush	2
Four-card flush	1
Low pair	3
Open-end four-card straight	1
Inside four-card straight (with high card)	1

Three-card straight flush	2
2 card royal, No. 10	3
3 high cards (Jacks or better)	2
2 high cards (Jacks or better)	3
None of the above	5

With video poker machines, this chapter will emphasize, it is crucial to know the differences between what machines offer.

Full-Pay Video Poker Pay Schedules

(Multiply payout below by 5 for the payout for maximum-coin play.)

Joker Wild

Royal flush	800
5 of a kind	200
Joker royal	100
Straight flush	50
4 of a kind	20
Full house	7
Flush	5
Straight	3
3 of a kind	2
2 pair	1
Pair (K-K)+	1
Payback 100.64%	

Deuces Wild

Natural royal flush	800
Four deuces	200
Wild royal flush	25
5 of a kind	15
Straight flush	9
4 of a kind	5
Full house	3
Flush	2
Straight	2
3 of a kind	1
Payback 100.76%	

9/6 Jacks+

Royal flush	800
Straight flush	0
4 of a kind	25
Full house	9
Flush	6

10/7 Double Bonus

Royal flush	800
Straight flush	50
Four aces	160
Four 5s-Ks	50
Four 2s, 3s, 4s	80

43

Straight	4		Full house	10
3 of a kind	3		Flush	7
2 pair	2		Straight	5
Jacks or better	1		3 of a kind	3
Payback 99.54%			Pair	1
			Jacks or better	1
			Payback 100.15%	

Below is a full-pay 9/6 regular VP pay schedule for Jacks or better with the value of one-coin and maximum-coin returns.

Pays: Jacks or Better (Jacks+) 9/6	one-coin return	max-coin return
Pair—jacks or better	returns the bet	5 coins
Two pair (2 PR)	pays 2-1	10 coins
Three of a kind (three of a kind)	pays 3-1	15 coins
Straight (ST) (sequence, not same suit)	pays 4-1	20 coins
Flush (FL) (nonsequential, same suit)	pays 6-1	30 coins
Full house (FH) (three of a kind and a pair)	pays 9-1	45 coins
Four of a kind (any)	pays 25-1	125 coins
Straight flush (SF) (in sequence, same suit)	pays 50-1	250 coins
Royal flush (RF)	pays 250-1	4,000 coins

This payout on the full house and flush is the method a casino generally uses to loosen or tighten a VP machine . . . and they even tell you! Isn't that great?

In a grouping of video poker machines, known as banks or carousels, all of which may look exactly the same, casinos will often mix in, as with slot placement, several VP machines with inferior pay programs. Most often in such a bank of regular, nonprogressive, non-bonus VP machines, only one or two may be the 9/6 types (nine coins for a full house, six coins for a flush).

In some casino areas, you will find only 8/5 Jacks or Better machines, which pay eight coins for a full house and five coins for a flush. These are not nearly as desirable as 9/6 VP machines. Even worse are the 7/5 machines. On cruise ships, the impossible 6/5 machines should be thrown overboard.

For 9/6 video poker, the expected loss playing five coins per hand is $13.20 per hour; 8/5 costs over $20 per hour; and lousy 6/5 VPs run over $30 per hour. Knowing which VP to play saves you $7 to $17 per hour.

What a difference these numbers make. A 6/5 machine has a low overall payback of 72 percent, versus 99.6 percent for the full-pay 9/6 machine.

You can see why your money will last a lot longer on a 9/6 machine. However, you might consider playing an 8/5 machine if it's a progressive (and most progressives are 8/5s) and the jackpot is much higher than usual for a royal flush.

If you bet five coins, all winning hands are paid out multiplied by a factor of five, except for the royal flush. This is a bonus amount designed as an incentive to play five coins. All those players who play less than the maximum number of coins are setting up the best payoffs for those who do.

The Top Ten VPs

Below is the average overall payback percentage for ten of the best VP versions. These percentages are maintained with the maximum number of coins per hand, "full-pay" schedule play, and perfect strategy.

1) 10/4 Loose Deuces—4 deuces pays 2,500=100.97%
2) 9/5 Deuces Wild=100.76%
3) 7/5 Jokers Wild—Five of a kind pays 1,000, quad pays 100=100.64%
4) 9/6 Double Double Jackpot Poker—2 pair pays 1=100.35%
5) 10/7 Double Bonus—2 pair pays 1=100.17%

6)   Pick Em Poker—pair of 9's or better minimum payout=99.95%
7)   11/7 Triple Bonus Poker—Kings or better minimum payout=99.94%
8)   9/6 Jacks+—2 pair pays 2=99.54 percent
9)   8/5 Bonus Jacks+—2 pair pays 2, four aces pays 400=99.17%
10) 9/6 Double Double Bonus—4 Aces with 2, 3, or 4 pays 2,000=98.98%

The first two numbers reflect the payouts for a full house and flush as per a one-coin payout. Therefore, a 10/7 Double Bonus, VP version No. 5, would pay ten coins for a full house and seven coins for a flush for a one-coin bet.

The exceptions to this are the Deuces Wild versions—No.1 and, No. 2—which reflect the payouts for a straight flush and four of a kind as per a one-coin payout. The minimum payout for a Deuces game is three of a kind.

The Jackpot version No. 4 is also known as Aces and Faces, where the higher payouts are reserved for aces, kings, queens, and jacks.

In addition, because Bonus VP versions offer higher payouts for four aces and four 2s, 3s, and 4s, the pair and two-pair payouts are often the same: one coin.

VP versions that pay two for two pair are Nos. 8 and 9, Jacks+ and Bonus Jacks+ in the guide above. It bears repeating that these percentages are maintained with maximum-coin, full-pay schedules and perfect strategy in play. The actual payout of any video poker machine is determined not only by its schedule but also by how you select your discards.

The best-paying VP machines also have a royal flush maximum-coin payoff of 4,000 coins—or the more rarely seen 4,700 coins. It takes some searching to find 4,700s, but they are on the floor in Nevada casinos and online.

In fact, although a VP player may experience more losing than winning sessions, this is offset by the royal flush payout—which a skilled player is more likely to get. I would be surprised to find one avid, skilled VP player who has not hit the big jackpot, wiping out the casino advantage in one swoop.

One item VP has in common with other slots is the RNG—the random number generator that constantly deals poker hands from a fifty-two-card deck. Since playing errors can reduce the payout, just sitting down in front of a full-pay machine won't help you unless you learn the correct strategies. With the dexterity or skill of making the right decisions for each VP version, this game is one of the best bets in the house.

With that task in mind, let's move on to strategies for several VP versions.

In VP, there are over two million possible hands. You will probably deal with only thirty or forty possibilities, so the Jacks or Better strategies are fairly simple.

<u>Jacks or Better (Jacks+)</u>

The strategy card for Jacks or Better VP shown earlier in this chapter will help. Full-pay 9/6 offers nine coins for a full house and six coins for a flush; on 8/5 machines, a full house pays eight and only five for a flush. You may think that five coins between a 9/6 and 8/5 version do not make much difference. Think again: You are now playing a short, or partial-pay, machine, and the casinos can do this legally, counting on the uneducated players not noticing the difference. You are looking at a 5 percent casino advantage with partial-pay machines.

- The ace is not the most important card here. A jack, queen, or king will also return your bet when paired. In addition, the jack, queen, or king offers more opportunities to develop winning hands around it than an ace does. For example, to form a sequence, a jack has two possibilities—a queen on one side and a 10 on the other. An ace, however, has only one face-card sequence partner, the king. (The deuce for a low straight is possible, but it is not a good drawing option.)
- Never keep a kicker—that's an additional face card—with any pair. To do so will reduce your return by 5 percent. Let that pair stand on its own and draw three cards.
- Always keep a five-card winning pat hand, with one exception: if you can draw one card to a royal flush.
- Don't break a flush even if you can draw one to a straight flush. However, always break a flush to draw one card to a royal flush.

- Never break a straight to draw to a straight flush. If you have three cards to a flush and no high cards, draw two cards for the flush.
- If you have four cards in succession for a straight, draw one card. Four consecutive cards is called an outside, or open-ended, straight when there are two possibilities for a winning hand, one at either end. So if you have 6-7-8-9, either a 5 or 10 will give you a winning hand. An inside, or gutshot, straight narrows your odds of completing that straight. For example, if you have 5-6-8-9, trying to get the 7 is called drawing to an inside straight, because the single card you need is on the inside. I suggest that you draw to an inside straight only if one of the other cards is a jack or better, where you can at least return your bet if you match that high card. Keep a small pair (jacks or less) for three of a kind.
- If all your cards are 10 or under with no possibility in sight for a winner, it's best to get five new cards.

In VP, 20 percent of all original first hands dealt are winners. A Jacks+ VP will generally hit the royal flush each 40,000 hands played, or every eighty to one hundred hours of play.

There are many Jacks+ Bonus VP versions to choose from today, and I discuss strategies for them under the Bonus Jacks+ VP heading.

Video poker with a full-pay 9/6 machine is one of my favorite games. However, Deuces Wild is an excellent second choice.

Deuces Wild

Unlike Jacks+ and Bonus VP, where the payout schedule is determined by the full house and flush, a Deuces Wild pay schedule is determined by the straight flush and four of a kind payouts.

Full-pay Deuces Wild pay schedules are 9/5 (nine coins for a straight flush and five for four of a kind, as listed under the one-coin payout schedule).

Partial-pay is 9/4, where only twenty coins are paid for four of a kind with the maximum number of coins in play.

Every five thousand hands of cycled play, on average, will produce four deuces—a secondary jackpot to the royal flush.

This is a game where less than perfect strategy can be very costly; however, when the game is played correctly, the return is 100.76 percent.

Newbie players are reluctant to throw away all five cards, but this is a most important strategy, in that you want to make room for additional cards that could be a deuces. Holding on to that ace or king is not going to help you if the next hand is destined to be four or five sevens. That explains why die-hard Jacks or Better players throw away a complete hand (five cards) only 3 percent of the time, while Deuces Wild players toss all five almost 20 percent of the time, nearly every fifth hand.

Below is a full-pay 9/5 VP pay schedule for Deuces Wild.

The minimum payout that qualifies for a return of your bet is three of a kind; therefore, you would not hold two pair, but choose one pair only to draw to.

The table below illustrates the payout for specific winning hands, one-coin return payout, and maximum-coin return payout.

Deuces 9/5 Hands	one-coin return	max-coin return
Three of a kind	pays 1-1	5 coins
Straight (sequence, not same suit)	pays 2-1	10 coins
Flush (nonsequential, same suit)	pays 2-1	10 coins
Full house (three of a kind and a pair)	pays 3-1	15 coins
Four of a kind (quad)	pays 5-1	25 coins
Straight flush (in sequence, same suit)	pays 9-1	45 coins
Five of a kind	pays 15-1	75 coins
Wild royal flush (includes deuces)	pays 25-1	125 coins
Four deuces	pays 200-1	1,000 coins

Royal flush (except with maximum coins)	pays 250-1	4,000 coins

I have simplified the basic strategies below; hold cards are determined by the number of deuces dealt for each hand, as follows:

4 Deuces Wild (DW): Hold all cards.

3DW: Hold wild royal flush, any high five of a kind (10s through aces). When you discard the lower cards (less than 10s), there are more high cards in the deck, therefore improving your chances of a wild royal or four deuces for a better payout.

2DW: Hold four of a kind or better, any four-card royal; or any suited open-ended straight flush (6 or higher). You would not hold a possible straight flush lower than 6, to form an A-2-3-4-5 straight flush, because you would lose the value of the deuce.

1DW: Hold pat hands, except to draw to a four-card royal; any four-card straight flush, including inside draws (remember, this is a wild-card game); or a three-card royal.

Hold ace high only if one or more of the other cards is of the same suit. For example, if you have the ace of spades and the jack of spades, then hold with the deuce.

Do not hold an ace and a jack if they're not same suit; that strategy will bring in a possible straight—no big money there.

Hold any two parts of a straight flush beginning with 6-7 or higher.

0DW: Hold any pat hand, except always draw to a four-card royal flush, four-card straight flush (including inside draw), three-card royal flush (see above for exceptions), one pair (discard the second pair—you do not have to keep the highest pair every time as any three of a kind pays), four-card flush, open four-card straight, three-card straight flush, and any inside draws (for example, J-10, Q-10, Q-J, K-10, K-J, K-Q, suited).

None of the above: all five cards are discarded.

To further simplify:

- Never hold one card except a deuce.
- Never hold two cards unless they're a pair or a two-card royal draw (exceptions noted above).
- Never hold three cards unless they're three of a kind, a straight flush, or a royal draw, and never, never hold just one other card with one, two, or three deuces. The sequence 7-J has the best straight and straight flush potentials.

Here are three recommended Deuces VP versions, along with strategies:

<u>Loose, Double, and Bonus Deuces</u>

The Loose Deuces VP version pay schedule generally reflects 10/4 and 11/4. This translates to ten or eleven coins for a straight flush and four for four of a kind.

The Loose Deuces pay schedule also reflects other hands that would be considered short pays, such as reducing five of a kind to sixty coins (seventy-five for full pay) and Wild Royals to one hundred (125 for full pay). However, the payoff of 2,500 coins for four deuces results in a total overall payback of 100.97 percent.

Double Deuces with a 2,000-coin payoff for Four Deuces results in a payback of 100.93 percent.

Two strategy changes for Double or Loose Deuces from regular 9/5 Deuces Wild play are noted: 1) three deuces are held alone, even discarding a wild royal, and 2) hold one pair rather than a four-card flush as you focus on the Deuces jackpot.

One of my favorites is Bonus Deuces Wild, which offers extra payouts of 2,000 coins for four deuces with an ace and higher coins for five of a kind. Five 6s, 7s, 8s, 9s 10s, Jacks, Queens or Kings to include one or more Deuces results in 100 credits. Five 3s, 4s or 5s to include one or more Deuces give you 200 credits, and five aces brings on 400 credits. The overall payout is 99.45 percent.

As you have learned by now, all Bonus VPs come with a price by shorting other hands. With this version, you are paid the same for three of a kind and straights; therefore, the strategy change here would be not to hold four parts of an inside or outside straight.

Jokers Wild

Jokers Wild is another popular wild-card game, but it requires alternative strategies, as fewer than 10 percent of your initial cards dealt will contain the joker.

The majority of your hands will look like those on a Jacks or Better machine, but don't fall into the trap of using the same Jacks or Better strategy play.

Below is a full-pay 7/5 VP pay schedule for Jokers Wild, kings or better.

The table below illustrates the payout for specific winning hands, showing one-coin return payout and maximum-coin return payout.

Jokers Wild 7/5 Hands	one-coin return	max-coin return
Pair—kings or better	returns the bet	5 coins
Two pair	returns the bet	5 coins
Three of a kind	pays 2-1	10 coins
Straight (sequence, not same suit)	pays 3-1	15 coins
Flush (FL) (non-sequential, same suit)	pays 5-1	25 coins
Full house (three of a kind and a pair)	pays 7-1	35 coins
Four of a kind (quad)	pays 20-1	100 coins
Straight flush (in sequence, same suit)	pays 50-1	250 coins
Joker royal (includes joker)	pays 100-1	500 coins
Five of a kind	pays 200-1	1,000 coins

Royal flush (except with maximum coins)	pays 250-1	4,000 coins

The average return for 7/5 Jokers Wild is 100.64 percent. This percentage is maintained with the maximum number of coins per hand at a full-pay machine with perfect strategy.

Strategy: First, and most important, the full-pay Jokers Wild pay schedules will be 7/5 machines, paying seven coins for a full house and five coins for a flush.

- A quad (four of a kind) pays 100 coins on a maximum-coin bet. This is important, as many 7/5 Joker games have a reduction to eighty or even the lowly seventy-five payout for quads.
- The two most available versions are 1) returns your bet with a pair of kings or better, and 2) requires at least two pair before any coin is paid. The stingy return here is 92.0 percent.
- The first version with payouts for a pair of kings or better allows the player an advantage; therefore, why would anyone play the other version? Additionally, the strategies for the two-pair minimum version are difficult to learn.
- As with Deuces Wild, the original five cards dealt are discarded more often than they are in Jacks or Better.

With Joker

- Hold pat hands of full house or better.
- Break a paying flush for a four-card royal or four-card open straight flush.
- Break three of a kind for any four-card straight flush.
- Break a pair of aces or kings for a three-card or better straight flush (must be consecutive) or any four-card flush.
- If none of the above apply, select a middle card (from 5 to 10) to keep with the joker.
- Barring a middle card, there may be times when you should hold

the joker alone. More than 3 percent of the time, you won't be able to connect with a straight, flush, straight flush, or a high pair. How ever, holding the joker alone can give you four new cards and a win.

Without Joker

- Hold two pair or better, but break a flush for any four-card royal draw and break a straight for any four-card straight flush or royal draw.
- Break a pair of aces or kings for any three-card royal draw.
- Break a low pair for four-card flush or an open-ended three-card straight flush.
- Break any pair for a four-card straight flush.
- Hold any four-card straight or any three-card straight flush, if consecutive, discarding a small pair in hopes of hitting the larger payout.
- Hold Ace and King of same suit.
- Hold suited faces K-Q, K-J, K-10, Q-J, Q-10, or J-10.
- Go for a straight flush whenever possible, for the larger return. With this wild-card game, straight flush and joker royal flush opportunities appear more often than in Jacks or Better.
- Keep a lower pair over the possibility of pulling a joker for a four-card straight, especially an inside straight. Although it is generally basic strategy in VP to hold an inside straight in wild-card games, in this case the payout for the straight has been reduced from four to three, so keep the pair only.

Some Vegas casinos have installed Jokers Wild with 4,700-coin royal flushes, a very good deal indeed.

Bonus Jacks or Better VP

The Video Poker world has exploded over the years, with more versions and takeoffs on those versions. Using Jacks or Better as the minimum payout, here are examples of pay schedules for Bonus VP, along with corresponding strategies.

Bonus and Double Bonus VP are two very popular versions.

This full-pay 8/5 Bonus Poker pay table illustrates the payout for specific winning hands, showing one-coin return payout, and maximum-coin return payout.

Bonus Poker 8/5 Hands	one-coin return	max-coin return
Pair—jacks or better	returns the bet	5 coins
Two pair	pays 2-1	10 coins
Three of a kind	pays 3-1	15 coins
Straight (sequence, not same suit)	pays 4-1	20 coins
Flush (FL) (non-sequential, same suit)	pays 5-1	25 coins
Full house (three of a kind and a pair)	pays 8-1	40 coins
Four of a kind (quad), 5s to kings	pays 25-1	125 coins
Four of a kind (quad) 2s, 3s, or 4s	pays 40-1	200 coins
Four aces	pays 80-1	400 coins
Straight flush (in sequence, same suit)	pays 50-1	250 coins
Royal flush (except with maximum coins)	pays 250-1	4,000 coins

Best Strategy: Hold two pair for the ten-coin payout. The ten-coin or 2-1 payout for two pairs will keep you in the game longer, and although a quad of 5s to kings pays out only 125, this game is suggested as a good bonus play for VP players moving up from regular Jacks or Better.

The average payback for Bonus Poker is 99.17 percent.

Up next is a full-pay 10/7 Double Bonus Poker pay table.

Double Bonus Poker 10/7 Hands	one-coin return	max-coin return
Pair—jacks or better	returns the bet	5 coins
Two pair	returns the bet	5 coins
Three of a kind	pays 3-1	15 coins
Straight (sequence, not same suit)	pays 5-1	25 coins
Flush (FL) (non-sequential, same suit)	pays 7-1	35 coins
Full house (three of a kind and a pair)	pays 10-1	50 coins
Four of a kind (quad) fives to kings	pays 50-1	250 coins
Four of a kind (quad) 2s, 3s, or 4s	pays 80-1	400 coin
Four aces	pays 160-1	800 coins
Straight flush (in sequence, same suit)	pays 50-1	250 coins
Royal flush (except with maximum coins)	pays 250-1	4,000 coins

Best Strategy: two pair should be saved for the possibility of a generous full-house payout of fifty coins. This VP game is the best bonus bet in the house.

Double Bonus Poker boasts a payback of 100.15 percent.

Following is a full-pay Double Double Bonus Poker pay table, which illustrates the payout for specific winning hands, showing one-coin return payout and maximum-coin return payout.

Double Double Bonus 9/6 Hand	one-coin return	max-coin return
Pair—jacks or better	returns the bet	5 coins
Two pair	returns the bet	5 coins
Three of a kind	pays 3-1	15 coins
Straight (sequence, not same suit)	pays 4-1	20 coins
Flush (FL) (non-sequential, same suit)	pays 6-1	30 coins
Full house (three of a kind and a pair)	pays 9-1	45 coins
Four of a kind (quad) fives to kings	pays 50-1	250 coins
Four of a kind (quad) 2s, 3s, or 4s	pays 80-1	400 coin
Four aces	pays 160-1	800 coins
Four of a kind 2s, 3s, 4s with A-4	pays 160-1	800 coins
Four aces with 2, 3, or 4	pays 400-1	2,000 coins
Straight flush (in sequence, same suit)	pays 50-1	250 coins
Royal flush (except with maximum coins)	pays 250-1	4,000 coins

Best Strategy: Keep your eye on the prize of four aces with a 2, 3, or 4 as a fifth card that pays out 2,000 coins—halfway to a royal.

- If dealt an ace with two face cards not of the same suit (example: jack of clubs and king of hearts), keep the ace only. This generous payday will occur approximately once every 16,000 hands.
- Pairs of aces, 2s, 3s, and 4s should be held for higher returns.

Warning: some casinos will lower the full-house or flush payout to 9/5 or the horrible 8/5, which should be avoided.

Note, too, that a straight is lowered to twenty coins for a maximum return vs. twenty-five coins for Double Bonus 10/7 versions.

Although this is a very popular VP version, do keep in mind that the total payback of 98.98 percent is not as high as Double Bonus 10/7 VP.

We now turn our attention to Double Double Jackpot Poker and Double Jackpot Poker. These versions are also known as Aces and Faces.

The Double Double Jackpot Poker version boasts the better overall average return of 100.35 percent when played with optimum strategy.

The tables below illustrate the payout for specific winning hands, showing one-coin return payout and maximum-coin return payout.

Double Double Jackpot Poker 9/6 Hands	one-coin return	max-coin return
Pair—jacks or better	returns the bet	5 coins
Two pair	returns the bet	5 coins
Three of a kind	pays 3-1	15 coins
Straight (sequence, not same suit)	pays 5-1	25 coins
Flush (FL) (non-sequential, same suit)	pays 6-1	30 coins
Full house (three of a kind and a pair)	pays 9-1	45 coins
Four of a kind (quad), 2s to 10s	pays 50-1	250 coins
Four of a kind (quad) kings, queens, jacks	pays 80-1	400 coin
Four of a kind (quad) KQJ with AKQJ	pays 160-1	800 coins
Four aces	pays 160-1	800 coins

Four aces with KQJ	pays 320-1	1,600 coins
Straight flush (in sequence, same suit)	pays 50-1	250 coins
Royal flush (except with maximum coins)	pays 250-1	4,000 coins

As you can see, the straight, at 25 coins, and the full house, at 45 coins, are more generous than most Bonus VP schedules. Generous, too, is the KQJ quads plus the four aces, with or without a fifth card.

There is not much of a strategy change for players with this game, as it's second nature to hold jacks or better with Bonus VP games; however, these versions offer a higher payout, so if you are dealt two pair, one pair being jacks or better, it is best to hold that one higher-paying pair to grab that quad payout.

The overall average payback is 100.35 percent.

Double Jackpot Poker 8/5 Hands	one-coin return	max-coin return
Pair—jacks or better	returns the bet	5 coins
Two pair	pays 2-1	10 coins
Three of a kind	pays 3-1	15 coins
Straight (sequence, not same suit)	pays 4-1	20 coins
Flush (FL) (non-sequential, same suit)	pays 5-1	25 coins
Full house (three of a kind and a pair)	pays 8-1	40 coins
Four of a kind (quad) 2s to 10s	pays 20-1	100 coins
Four of a kind (quad), kings, queens, jacks	pays 40-1	200 coins

Four of a kind (quad) KQJ with AKQJ	pays 80-1	400 coins
Four aces	pays 80-1	400 coins
Four aces with KQJ	pays 160-1	800 coins
Straight flush (in sequence, same suit)	pays 50-1	250 coins
Royal flush (except with maximum coins)	pays 250-1	4,000 coins

This version is definitely a poor imitation of its cousin, discussed above; however, the better A-K-Q-J quad payouts remain. The straight and full house are reduced by five coins, but two pair is increased to ten with maximum coins in play.

Holding both pairs, regardless of card rank, is best here so that you collect at least the ten-coin reward and stay in the game.

The overall average payback is a respectable 99.63 percent.

More VP Choices

Multi play: As in standard video poker, you're dealt five cards and may hold from zero to five. The difference is that the cards you hold appear in all the other hands.

These versions now appear with three, five, ten, fifty, and even one hundred hands per bet.

A hefty bankroll is required; a quarter, five-play machine can cost you a bet of $6.25 per spin ($1.25 x 5 = $6.25).

Rarely will you find full-pay VP pay schedules on multi plays, except in higher denominations; however, when you do, I recommend them.

The Game Maker multidenomination machines offer two other highly rated VP versions in some casinos: Pick 'Em Poker and All American Poker.

The Pick 'Em Poker VP version allows the player to "build" a hand. You are dealt two cards and must select from two stacks of three cards to complete your hand; however, only the top card is visible.

All-American Poker is the only VP version I know that gives the straight flush the respect it deserves by paying out 1,000 credits for this often elusive hand.

Also, straights, flushes, and full houses all pay out forty credits.

Optimal strategy is more complicated with this version than with others, but here are a few tips:

- Keep two pair for the full-house payout.
- Keep two parts of a royal flush.
- Keep four parts of a flush rather than a small pair.
- Keep four parts of an inside or outside straight for the forty credits.

This game is well worth the extra study and homework!

Video Poker—Newer Versions

Below is a list of newer Video Poker versions for 2007 and beyond.

I offer a caveat here: Most of the time—but not all of the time, thankfully—newer versions do not have better pay schedules than the standards, so approach them cautiously. I list one of the better versions at the bottom of this list.

Except for one VP game, all versions are by IGT, which manufactures the only VP game in town and literally owns the marketplace for land-based casinos.

1) Draw 6 Poker: The unusual twist here is that your get three extra cards, not two, when you are dealt three of a kind.

2) Back It Up Poker: When you have four of a kind or a straight flush in one hand, the next hand will pay out fives times the normal credits if you repeat.

3) Ace Invaders: Similar to Triple Play, with a twist. The similar part is the bottom-line deal, while the top two lines are played with no draw and a full fifty-two-card deck for each. The fun part is that aces at the top can be matched with the bottom two lines for bonus credits.

4) Five Play Multi-Strike: If you like Multi-Strike, you will love this Five Play version, which offers the added incentive of climbing to the top

line approximately every second game, as opposed to every eight hands with the original single-payline version.

5)   Big Times Draw Poker: A multiplier is an integral part of this game available in Triple, Five, and Ten Play at a wager of ten coins per line. Each line includes a multiplier ranging from one to ten triggered by the highest-ranking card in the hand. It's interesting to note that face cards rank higher than the low-end ace, receiving a one multiplier, while a full house or quad with kicker, or fifth card, rewards with a ten multiplier.

6)   Hold 'Em Challenge: This is a slot version of the popular poker game (the so-called Cadillac of poker) regularly seen on TV.

7)   Max Out Poker is my favorite on this list. You play eight coins on this four-line version—five coins for the bottom line and one coin each for the top three lines.

The bottom line will pay for pairs and/or three of a kind for the Deuces version.

However, with the top three lines, you aren't paid for pairs, but the "top-heavy" payouts are found with increased coins for quads, straight flushes, and royals.

The higher pays for the top three lines necessitates a change in strategy: You will hold three parts of a straight flush versus. a pair, three parts of a royal versus a pair, three of a kind versus four parts of a straight.

Optimal play requires that you reach as often as possible for the higher payouts while paying attention to the schedules for the top three lines.

Because there are a wide variety of VP versions with different pay schedules offered for Max Out Poker, I have compiled a list of the top ten versions. Normally, I do not advocate newer versions, but no serious VP player should ignore 99.0+ VP games.

Maximum-Payout Schedule Return

Rank	VP Version	Average Pay
1)	Bonus Poker Deluxe 9/6	100.14 percent
2)	Super Aces Bonus Poker 8/5	100.09 percent

3)	Deuces Wild Poker 25/16/10/4	100.01 percent
4)	Jacks+ 9/6	99.97 percent
5)	Super Double Double Bonus 8/5	99.94 percent
6)	White Hot Aces 9/5	99.86 percent
7)	Joker Poker 7/5 Kings+ (18 for quad)	99.59 percent
8)	Bonus Poker 8/5	99.48 percent
9)	Double Bonus Poker 9/7/5	99.35 percent
10)	Double Double Bonus 9/6/4	99.29 percent

Deuces Wild Strategy: If dealt five of a kind with three deuces, keep only the deuces.

Note: The maximum-payout percentage is maintained with the maximum number of coins per hand at a full-pay machine with optimal strategy.

General VP Notes and Tips

- Progressives are usually 8/5s as approximately 1 percent of the money taken in goes toward the ever-growing royal flush jackpot; consequently, the other payouts suffer. Thus, as stated before, VP should always be played with the maximum number of coins. Let me share an instructive anecdote about this. At one Vegas casino, the Megapoker machines were offering a $29,000 jackpot. The big jackpot was hit quickly the first time, but management noticed that the second big payoff was slow in coming. Some little jackpots were paid out, but not the top prize. The managers scratched their heads and wondered what was happening. Then they discovered the reason for the lack of another jackpot: Gamblers were not playing the maximum number of coins. Can you imagine—these players were one or two coins away from twenty-nine grand. Oh, the horror of it all! Please remember this story when you are tempted to play only three coins in a five-coin machine.
- If you can't afford to play five coins at a quarter VP, play five coins on a nickel VP, as the royal flush pays out $200. The same royal flush with just one quarter in play will get you only $62.50 (250 credits) on a

63

quarters VP—easy decision here. Some players' strategy is to play for the royal flush only. I don't agree with this, as it takes a large bank roll and shortens your playing time. But with basic strategy, small wins can keep you playing—without affecting your wager-management plan—while leading up to that royal flush jackpot.

- Keep an eye on that screen for lit payouts or win announcements. I find that new players do not always notice that they have a winning hand right in front of their nose.

Here are two misconceptions about VP:

Misconception No. 1: Playing fast or with two hands will make the machine pay out more often.

This is not a good idea because it leads to mistakes. Besides, the computer will not let you go any faster before a new hand is dealt. What's your hurry, anyway? Study each hand carefully before you make your discard decision.

Misconception No. 2: If the next player wins on a machine that you have just played, he or she took "your win."

Just as in slots, this is not the way things work. It's just the way the RNG bounces.

A friend of mine left a VP machine and went to another 9/6 machine down the row. Five minutes later, a fellow hit the royal flush on her previous machine. He pointed at her and said, in a loud voice, "This was your machine!" Then he crossed his arms and waited for the attendant. He seemed to take so much glee in thinking that it had been her machine and now it was his. My friend didn't bother to tell him that he might have played one or more cards differently.

She knew the RNG explanation was not worth mentioning, either.

To her credit, she simply turned to him and said, "Good for you. Congratulations." Jim, my husband, and I have a plan. We divide up the different types of machines and each play what we know.

This works well for us, as we are pooling our bankroll and VP knowledge. Practice at home is mandatory. Since I started using VP tutoring software, my strategy knowledge has increased immensely, to the point that I can easily move among most VP models with confidence.

I take a few minutes to focus when changing from Bonus machines to Deuces or Jokers Wild, but the increased knowledge makes me a true student of the game. In the ever-changing VP world, it's especially important to practice and study new games as they appear.

As exciting as video poker is, there's nothing like live action, sitting with your fellow players across from a live dealer. Among casino card games, by far the most popular of these over the years has been blackjack, or 21.

In addition to being pure adrenaline, it's one of the best values in the casino! Turn to the next chapter for more information.

How to Win at Blackjack

7

For a player who has mastered basic strategy, blackjack tables, under specific conditions, offer an opportunity to compete on a level playing field with the casino. This makes 21 as good a betting situation as the informed gambler can find.

For those new to the game, the rules and basic terms of the game are as follows:

- Your cards add up to points, and 21 wins. Whoever comes closest—you or the dealer—to a total of 21 points without going over ("busting" or "breaking"), wins.
- An ace counts as 1 point or 11 points. Face cards all count as 10 points. All other cards count as marked.
- Hard hand: A hand that does not include an ace. What you see on your two cards is your total count; for example, $9 + 8 = 17$.
- Soft hand: A hand that includes an ace in the first two cards dealt. It has two values, depending on whether you count the ace as a 1 or an 11. For instance, a 5 and an ace could be 6 or 16. A 10 turns a soft hand into a hard hand.
- Stiff hand: A potential bust hand, such as a 13 or 14, but especially a hard 15 or 16, which are the two worst hands you can get (unless the 16 is two 8s, in which case you can and should split them into two hands).
- Split or Splitting Pairs: Splitting a matched pair to play separately.

The extra bet is placed on one of the split cards. If a third like card is dealt, that too can be split based on casino rules.

- Splitting Aces: When you split aces, you receive only one additional card for each hand. However, based on casino rules you may split a third ace if dealt.
- Double Down or Doubling Down: Doubling the bet before being dealt one additional card. The blackjack rule for doubling down is that the player receives only one card after a DD decision. Player may bet up to his or her original bet, but not more, and places this second bet behind the original bet. Some casinos allow doubling down only with a count of 10 or 11.
- Push: When you end up with the same count as the dealer. Same as a tie. No money is exchanged because you neither win nor lose.
- Burn cards: The number of cards the casino discards at the beginning of a new shuffle.
- Multiple decks: Four or more decks played in a game. They are always dealt faceup.
- Single or double decks: Only one or two decks played in a game. The first two cards are dealt facedown.

Blackjack has one of the best bottom-line advantages for the gambler with a high Intelligent Gambling Quotient. It's a sad fact that the casino's booming profits at blackjack tables are the result of poor player strategy. So let's fix that right now.

Going with your instincts in this game doesn't help you, but it sure helps the casino! In fact, it gives the casino a 5 percent advantage. That's too far above the 3 percent casino edge that any informed gambler should allow.

Mastering basic strategy brings that percentage down to 0.5 percent to 1 percent for the casino. The casino still holds a slight edge because the player has to draw first and could bust. However, with strategies such as tracking aces or keeping track of the high cards already out, you can bring this percentage close to 0 percent.

You gotta love that number!

On most blackjack layouts, you will notice these two statements: "Blackjack Pays 3 to 2" and "Insurance Pays 2 to 1." A pay of 3-2 means that a $10 bet pays $15. When the dealer's up card is an ace, there will be a call for insurance. If you make an insurance bet that the dealer has blackjack, this wager is placed on the insurance line displayed on the felt. If the dealer has blackjack, you win the insurance bet (pays 2-1); however, your original bet is lost. If there is no blackjack, you lose the insurance bet. The insurance bet is not recommended.

In addition, all blackjack layouts will have one of the two following statements: "Dealer Must Draw to 16 and Stand on All 17s" or "Dealer Must Hit Soft 17."

The first statement, "Dealer Must Draw to 16 and Stand on All 17s," is known as a player advantage layout and is shown in the illustration accompanying this chapter.

This is a typical layout of a blackjack table on the Las Vegas "Strip." Notice that the dealer must stand on *all* 17's. "All" 17's means that any total of 17, including an ace counted as 11 such as ace-6, stops the draw. This rule favors the player.

The second statement, "Dealer Must Hit Soft 17," is a player disadvantage layout.

The best blackjack tables show the "Dealer Must Draw to 16 and Stand on All 17s" statement, use a single deck, have no restrictions on doubling down, allow resplitting, and have a surrender option available. All these conditions favor the player.

When it can be found without severe conditions attached (such as dealer wins on a push or a reduced payout for blackjack—always check on such conditions), the single deck is the best bet in the casino. You are much more easily able to see when your chances are increased for being dealt a natural blackjack, or 21, and when you are dealt a blackjack there's an even better chance that the dealer will not tie this natural with one of his or her own.

In addition, a dealer standing on all 17s—especially soft 17s (a 17 count that includes an ace)—keeps the dealer from developing his or her hand any further, while retaining the player's option to do so.

With no restrictions on doubling down, you can press your bet up to the amount of your original wager on any two cards—not just 10 or 11, as in some blackjack games. I know players who double down on everything, but I don't recommend that strategy. However, you should certainly consider doubling down when you have an 8 or a 9, depending on what the dealer has showing.

The resplitting option helps you, too. Upon splitting once, you have the opportunity to wager on a third card of the same number. This can happen, for example, when you split two aces and a third is dealt. Only one hit is allowed on each split. Finally, with the surrender option (which is not always available), you can surrender after receiving your first two cards and lose only half of your original bet. Clearly say to the dealer, "Surrender," then fold your cards and sit out the rest of the hand.

In an early surrender, the player forfeits his or hand before the dealer checks for a blackjack. This is rare but has the best advantage for the player.

In a late surrender, the player forfeits his or her hand after the dealer has checked for a blackjack.

The best time to surrender is when you have 15 or 16 and the dealer's up card is 7 or higher. Except for the dealer-17 rule, the other options of player advantage conditions are not always advertised at the table. You have to double-check on these with the dealer.

Unless you are dealt a made hand (a hand of 17 or higher), in blackjack your primary consideration is the dealer's up card. Your main objective is not to get as close to 21 as possible but to beat the dealer.

It's very possible to win with a 13 or 14 count, if the dealer breaks.

I like the 7-up rule. If the dealer shows 2 through 6, and your have 13 through 16, always stand.

Other basic strategy is as follows:

- If the dealer shows 2 or 3 and you have 12, you should take a card. The rationale behind the 7-up rule is that the dealer has to hit anything up to 16 and could bust. It's better that the dealer bust than that you do.
- On the other hand, if the dealer's up card is a 7 or higher, always hit.
- Always stand on 17 or higher.
- Double down on 11 with no exceptions.
- Double down on 10 only when the dealer shows a 2 through 9. You get one card only.
- Always split aces and 8s. You get only one card on the aces and you determine the number of hits on the 8s, creating double-down options with 2 or 3.
- Never split 4s, 5s or 10s, because you already have an excellent hand. Two 4s are 8, and all you need is a 10 for 18. Two 5s give you a count of 10.
- Most players would love to get a 10 dealt first, so keep it. Two 10's give you an excellent hand of 20. Besides, who needs those stares you'd get from the dealer and other players if you split 10s?
- On splits and resplits, don't forget to play the same hit-or-stand strategies that you used with your original hand.

Below I have provided three basic sheets of blackjack strategy.

For best results at the blackjack tables, these tables should be memorized. Or you may photocopy them and ask the casino for permission to consult them at the table. Many casinos allow this. Some even provide simple "cheat sheets" with basic strategy.

Strategy for Multiple-Deck Blackjack

Basic Strategy for Hard Hands

Dealer's Up Card

Player	2	3	4	5	6	7	8	9	T	A
17	S	S	S	S	S	S	S	S	S	S
16	S	S	S	S	H	H	H	H	H	H
15	S	S	S	S	H	H	H	H	H	H
14	S	S	S	S	H	H	H	H	H	H
13	S	S	S	S	H	H	H	H	H	H
12	H	H	S	S	H	H	H	H	H	H
11	D	D	D	D	D	D	D	D	D	H
10	D	D	D	D	D	D	D	D	H	H
9	H	D	D	D	H	H	H	H	H	H
8	H	H	H	H	H	H	H	H	H	H

H=Hit. S=Stand. D=Double if allowed; if not, hit.

Basic Strategy for Soft Hands

Dealer's Up Card

Player	2	3	4	5	6	7	8	9	T	A
(A,9)	S	S	S	S	S	S	S	S	S	S
(A,8)	S	S	S	S	S	S	S	S	S	S
(A,7)	S	D or S	D or S	D or S	D or S	S	S	H	H	H
(A,6)	H	D	D	D	D	H	H	H	H	H
(A,5)	H	H	D	D	D	H	H	H	H	H
(A,4)	H	H	D	D	D	H	H	H	H	H
(A,3)	H	H	H	D	D	H	H	H	H	H
(A,2)	H	H	H	D	D	H	H	H	H	H

H=Hit. S=Stand. D=Double if allowed; if not, hit. D or S=Double if allowed; if not, stand.

Basic Strategy for Pair Splitting

Dealer's Up Card

Player	2	3	4	5	6	7	8	9	T	A
(A,A)	Y	Y	Y	Y	Y	Y	Y	Y	Y	Y
(T,T)	N	N	N	N	N	N	N	N	N	N
(9,9)	Y	Y	Y	Y	Y	N	Y	Y	N	N
(8,8)	Y	Y	Y	Y	Y	Y	Y	Y	Y	Y
(7,7)	Y	Y	Y	Y	Y	Y	N	N	N	N
(6,6)	Y	Y	Y	Y	Y	N	N	N	N	N
(5,5)	N	N	N	N	N	N	N	N	N	N
(4,4)	N	N	N	Y	Y	N	N	N	N	N
(3,3)	Y	Y	Y	Y	Y	Y	N	N	N	N
(2,2)	Y	Y	Y	Y	Y	Y	N	N	N	N

Y=Split the pair. N=Don't split.

Wager-Management Reminder: Blackjack is a streaky, up-and-down game. A skilled and serious player should have fifty bets in their session stake and four hundred units as their overall bankroll investment.

Progressive betting is definitely the road to profit; however, do not double your bet after every win. Smart players increase their bets maybe 20 to 30 percent at a time. Change some red $5 chips for white $1 chips if you have to. Instead of pressing or upping your bet from five bucks to ten, bet seven dollars, and get some $1 chips to make this bet.

Take note that table games in casinos are famous for coloring up, which means that instead of passing the player five $5 chips, they are given a $25 chip, a sneaky and nasty ploy on the casino's part. I give it back to the dealer and ask for change in five $5 chips; you usually only have to do that once, and the dealer will get the idea.

Get into the practice of general card counting. Start slowly by tracking the little cards, 2 through 6. If you see ten cards on the table and more than four of them are small, the player has an edge at that moment. The dealer's edge kicks in if there are fewer than four small cards. After a few hands, you'll have some feel for the deck, and this can help you to decide when to increase or decrease your bet.

Strict card counting is difficult to apply, illegal, and punishable, but you can still benefit from employing and acting on a rough count, or by learning what is called a plus or minus system. In this system, the low cards (2 through 6) have a value of +1, while the face cards and aces have a value of -1. The 7s, 8s and 9s are neutral and count as 0. If you keep track of all the cards in play using this system, you will have a running "count." When the total is a plus number, you have the advantage. If it's a minus number, the dealer has the advantage.

If you can snag the seat just before the dealer, on his or her righthand side, you can best survey the other cards before making your betting decisions. Pit crews are always on the lookout for expert card counters, so don't be too obvious! Vary your progressive bets. If card counting is suspected, the result could be a sudden reshuffle of the deck or a new dealer.

If you have taken the time to notice and compliment a dealer, don't blow it with an overzealous progressive bet that gives you away as a card counter.

In the rare situations where dealers look at their cards, especially checking for blackjack, you should watch for dealer "tells." These are signals that can help you. For instance, if you have a borderline decision to make and the dealer holds the cards close to his or her body or upward when asking if you want a card, it may be a signal that you should not take a card. The reverse is when the dealer almost hovers or leans toward you. Take that card!

These tells are rare bonuses. Don't forget to tip or "toke" for a good dealer.

Research has shown that female dealers (especially young females) are friendlier and may perhaps give better signals, or tells. I am simply repeating this information, not disputing it one way or another and will not comment on it further. How's that for fence-sitting?

At this juncture, I will toss in some useful blackjack stats:

- The dealer will bust about once every four hands played (28 percent). The player will be dealt a blackjack about once every twenty-one hands.
- The player who is dealt a hand of 18 will lose more often than win.
- For tables that allow the dealer to hit a soft 17, the casino's hold percentage shoots up to 6 percent from 2.6 percent if the dealer stands on all 17s.

There will always be die-hard blackjack players, and in some respects the game is still the best bet in the casino, and one of only a few games played around the world; however, the blackjack player does have other options, such as mini-baccarat, craps, pai gow poker, and live poker, where low house advantages await you as well.

I have one final suggestion for low rollers at blackjack. Some casino blackjack tables will raise the minimum over $10 in the evenings and on weekends. If you are already seated at the table, you should be allowed to continue at the previous minimum stakes. (You are "grandfathered" in.) But if you arrive late, do not feel forced to play for more than your budget allows. Instead, consider heading for the video blackjack machines, where you can play with quarters.

Or you can head in the direction of the loudest tables in the casino, where even the dealers are yelling!

You can head for the craps table.

Winning Ways at the Craps Table

8

This game brings out the emotions more than any other. At the craps table, you are free to applaud, cheer, and let loose. Many gamblers, especially women, are less intimidated by this game. Although the game layout looks complicated, craps is remarkably simple. To the educated gambler, it's even simpler, because he or she knows that there are only three major bets to consider, and following these slashes the casino's advantage down to less than 1 percent.

As you check out the table, note the minimum bet and the odds posted. Do these numbers fit into your wager-management plan? See how the dice are running. Is the money on come bets, place bets, or pass-line bets? Are these the features you want?

Still a little frightened?

Well, let me tell you how I started my craps education. About ten years ago, my brother tried to teach me the game. I wasn't retaining the information and, to tell the truth, I felt overwhelmed. I decided that the easiest way to make money was to make the same bets as my brother, who was on a winning streak. He reached down to make a bet and, of course, I followed, putting my hand down just as the shooter was flinging the dice. Well, my hand and the dice met, canceling the roll of a shooter who was blazing hot.

Dice shooters are among the most superstitious people in the world. Silence fell around the table.

I think the group of players was secretly planning revenge. I quietly exited, red-faced, while my brother denied any family connection.

A couple of years later, after observing the electricity of the game whenever I was in a casino, my determination to get educated kicked in. With the basic techniques memorized, I approached a craps table in Reno. I was the lone player (hey, not all my confidence had returned yet) and proceeded to make four passes in a row. A "pass" means that you hit your number, or win your bet, as explained below. I picked up my winnings and tipped and thanked the dealer, who told me no one else had thrown four in a row that day.

If I can do it, anyone can.

Basic Rules of Craps, and Some Craps Lingo

When a player is handed the dice to throw, the first roll is called a "come-out" roll. A 7 or 11 (known on the come-out roll as a "natural") wins immediately, while a 2, 3, or 12 (craps) loses immediately. Any other number has no pass-line significance. That is, the numbers 4, 5, 6, 8, 9, and 10 do not win or lose right away. Instead, they become "points," or numbers that, in order to win, must be repeated before a 7 is rolled.

This is why the 7 sometimes wins and sometimes loses, but always determines the outcome of a pass-line wager. If it's thrown on the first roll, it wins. But if it's thrown when the player tries to repeat his first-roll number, it loses. That is called a 7-out. Then it's the next player's turn to shoot. A shooter retains the dice as long as he or she continues to make passes or wins, either immediately on the come-out with a 7 or 11, or by repeating the point number successfully. The player keeps the dice even if he or she loses on the come-out roll with a 2, 3, or 12.

The player loses the dice only after a 7-out. This is the pass-line bet that's the most popular bet at the table and the first recommended wager.

The pass line extends around both ends of the table. Place your pass-line bet directly in front of you. This is important because you need the dealer's assistance to place additional bets.

The dealer will place the bet in the correct box in relation to where you are standing at the table. Don't worry; there are four casino staff members at every table, so your bet won't get lost.

Each end of the table has an identical layout, and each end has a dealer for eight players. It's ideal to arrive at a table when a shooter is coming out. You'll know this from the position of the puck, which says ON at the white side and OFF at the black side.

If the shooter made a point on the come-out roll and is now trying to repeat that number, the dealer will place the puck with the white ON side toward the rear center of the box that corresponds to the number (4, 5, 6, 8, 9, or 10).

If the shooter is trying for a 6, the puck will be in the 6 box with its ON side showing. However, if you notice the puck with the black side OFF in the don't-come area, that means the next roll is a come-out.

This is your signal to make that pass-line bet.

And when the shooter wins, everyone on the pass line wins.

Winning is even sweeter when you have backed up your pass-line bet with an odds bet placed directly behind it.

This odds bet is made only after a shooter has established a point and, statistically, it is the only bet in the casino where the house's edge is 0 percent. You receive the "true odds" for your wager.

But, you say, the layout has no space for an odds bet.

That's because the casino doesn't advertise odds bets. (And could that be because a ten times odds bet slashes the advantage of the original come-out roll to .2 percent? Double odds come down to .63 percent for the casino.)

Probabilities Chart

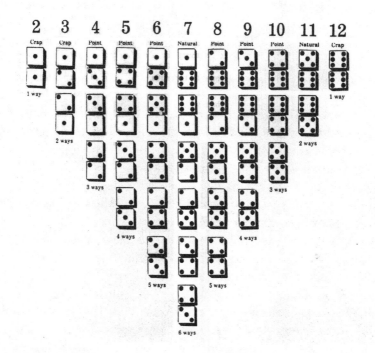

The odds bets are determined by a probability chart and are based on the thirty-six possible combinations that rolling two dice can produce. For instance, the 7 can be rolled six ways; it has the highest probability of occurring. The 6 and 8 can be rolled five ways, the 5 and 9 can be rolled four ways, and the 4 and 10 can be rolled three ways each.

Here's a little memory work for you. This information will become second nature and is essential for your craps education.

We will group the point numbers in sets. The payouts are for backing up, or "pressing," a come-out line bet:

6 and 8	6-to-5 odds	Pays $6 for every $5 wagered.
5 and 9	3-to-2 odds	Pays $3 for every $2 wagered.
4 and 10	2-to-1 odds	Pays $2 for every $1 wagered.

The table layout is grouped in the same way, with the 6 and 8 in the middle, the 5 and 9 one space over on either side, and the 4 and 10 at the far end. (See illustration below):

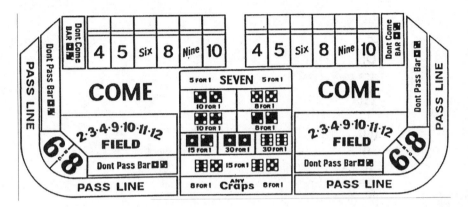

The casino pays on correct odds bets but not on a pass-line bet, which pays even money. It is simple to calculate double, triple, or even ten-times odds, which are very popular in Vegas. Sam's Town and the Horseshoe in Vegas has offered one-hundred-times odds—now, that's important!

Let's go over these odds one more time. Think 6 to 5 for 6 and 8; 3 to 2 for 5 and 9; and 2 to 1 for the end numbers, 4 and 10.

Most players use red $5 chips for the odds. If your bankroll allows for this, go for it.

It's important to repeat using $5 chips because if you do not take the correct odds with the right amount of chips, you will be paid even money only. The whole idea behind taking odds is for bigger wins. If you don't memorize this information, just ask the dealer, "What is the correct odds amount?" and follow those instructions.

The second optimum bet at a craps table is another two-step bet with odds well under that low, low 1 percent advantage for the casino.

It's the come bet, boldly displayed on the layout.

For this bet, you place the chips near your position on the table, while the shooter is trying to repeat a point number.

Think of this bet as a delayed pass-line bet, a new come-out roll with the same rules. It's like a game within a game after the original point has been established.

A come bet is also known as an insurance bet for your pass-line bet.

Let's say 6 has been established as the shooter number to win on the pass line, and you want an additional bet working for you. Okay, make that same bet as described in the come-bet area. If the next roll is a 9, you will be looking for a 6 "on the line" and a 9 "coming," before a 7 rolls.

If the next roll is a craps, you lose the come bet. A 7 or 11 wins outright, but remember the 7 wipes out the pass-line bet and all other pass-line wagers. In this case, the dealer places the payoff directly beside your bet. It's your responsibility to immediately pick up the chips. If your come bet is a point number, the dealer will position that bet for you.

Now comes the second part—making the odds bet to lower the casino advantage. Position this bet near the original come bet and, loud and clear, say to the dealer, "Odds on my come bet."

At any time, you can remove odds bets (but not pass-line or come bets, since they become points after the original role).

Lastly, the third bet is the place bet. It can be made any time after a point is established. The place bet on a 6 or 8 has a casino advantage of 1.5 percent.

Wagers must be made in multiples of $6 because the payoff is $7 for every $6 bet. It's very important that you clearly state your desire to make a place bet and have the dealer place the 6 or 8 for you. Do not confuse the place bet with the big 6 or 8 that is prominent on the layout. That is even money and has a casino advantage of 9 percent.

Place bets can be taken off at any time, and the bets are off on a come-out roll. When a place bet is won, the dealer will hand you your winnings only. If you want it all back, tell the dealer to take down the 6 or 8.

Let me add a wager-management recommendation here: Keep your minimum pass-line bet the same. Save the parlay (progressive betting) for betting odds double, triple, or whatever the table will allow. That's where your house advantage is low. At this point, if you've studied the layout, you're probably asking, "But what about all those other bets, like the field and proposition bets?"

Stay away from them.

They are all sucker bets, with anywhere from a 4 percent to a 16.7 percent house advantage.

Keep in mind that casino management trains dealers to sell these bets big-time.

I realize that there's a lot of action and excitement at the craps tables and that it's easy to get caught up in it all. But don't start throwing your money at dealers who give you a hard sell on these bets. Focus on the educated bets, the ones with the lowest house advantage: pass-line bets, come bets with odds on each, and 6 or 8 place bets. You'll get plenty of action making these educated bets. Mix and match them as you like, secure in the knowledge that you are hacking away at the casino advantage.

There are, however, a couple of other bets you might want to consider: the don't-pass and don't-come bets. These are sometimes called "wrong bets" (versus pass-line and come bets, which are called "right bets").

Wrong bets still keep you in that low, 1 percent casino-advantage range. But they can be risky and are not the most popular bets. Some players think they are playing for the house. But it's the house that pays when you win a wrong bet.

I make no apologies for recommending wrong bets, because you know you're going to run into cold craps tables and this is the only game where a losing streak can give you a betting advantage. With any other game, a run of losses will make you hurry away.

As you make wrong bets, my best advice is to stand near the don't-pass and don't-come areas on the table and maintain a low profile as you make a "don't" bet. When you win, keep in mind that a lot of other players at the table have lost. When a right bettor makes an odds bet, it's called taking the odds; but a wrong bettor is "laying the odds." In other words, on a don't-pass bet for a 4 and 10, I must lay $2 to win $1. I call that a backward bet.

A commission known as a "vig," or vigorish, of 5 percent is payable to the casino on all lay bets.

Nick the Greek was probably the best-known wrong bettor. What, you might ask, makes a wrong bet good? Just go back to that probability chart.

In the example of a don't-pass bet for a 4 and 10, we lose only if the point is rolled, and a 4 can be rolled in only three ways.

However, I will win with a 7, which can be rolled six ways.

In this example, the probability that a 7 will be rolled before a 4 or 10 is two to one in my favor. For a 5 or 9, the odds are three to two in my favor, while a 6 or 8 is six to five in my favor. This makes the don't-come wager the best 'wrong bet' I know. The 7, which is rogue to the right bettor, is hero to the wrong bettor. The debate continues.

You should not bet the don't-pass when you are the shooter, because you will be betting against yourself. That's never a problem for me, because I always pass when given the chance to be the shooter. You see, my pitching arm is not so great.

One time, I nearly hit a nearby blackjack player with the dice! As they say, "On the wood, no good... on the floor, out the door." I haven't been thrown out of a casino yet, but I don't want to take any chances. So I find that, for me, it's best to pass the dice. For anyone else, I certainly recommend taking a turn at shooting. This is an audience-participation game of the highest degree.

The best way to throw the dice is to pretend that you are tossing a cupful of water to the other end of the table, making sure that the dice bounce off that end of the table.

As for me, I think I'll just keep practicing at home.

Betting Tips Summary

- Keep your pass-line or don't-pass bet to the table minimum.
- Use progressive betting when taking or giving odds. That's where the real money is won.
- Don't make any craps (field or proposition) bets.
- Always repeat a winning parlay bet.
- Don't advance in your betting progression until you win two parlays in a row or win with odds.
- Best craps bets: A house edge under 3 percent is any intelligent player's goal.
- Pass-line bets: 1.41 percent

- Don't-pass bets: 1.40 percent
- Come bets: 1.41 percent
- Don't-come bets: 1.40 percent
- Place 6 and 8 to win: 1.51 percent

Multiple odds blow the house's edge away:

Single odds: 0.85 percent
Double odds: 0.61 percent
Triple odds: 0.47 percent
5 x odds: 0.32 percent
10 x odds: 0.18 percent.

Craps Terms: Get This Lingo, Folks!

Ace caught a loose deuce: number 3.
Ace-deuce: wagering that the next roll will total 3.
Aces: wagering that the next roll will total 2.
After five, the field's alive: wagering that the next roll will total 5.
All the spots we got: wagering that the next roll will total 12.
Atomic craps: wagering that the next roll will total 12.
Back-line skinner: wagering that the next roll will be a 7.
Ballerina special: wagering that the next roll will total 4.
Big red: placing a bet on any 7.
Bones: lingo for dice.
Boxcars: lingo for the number 12 or wagering that the next roll will be 12.
Brooklyn forest: looking for a hard 6.
Buffalo: placing a wager on each of the hardways and any 7.
Capped dice: lingo for crooked dice at the craps table.
Center field: wagering that the next roll will total 9.
Cold dice: this craps table has gone cold and the dice ain't passing. Also called "Cold Table."
Department of the Interior: craps player makes an inside bet.
Die in the wood, roll no good: whoa, the dice has hit a player's chip rack.

85

Double saw on boxcars: wagering that the next roll will total 12.

Easy way: numbers 4, 6, 8, or 10 rolled without pairs. Opposite of hardways.

End of the race: wagering that the next roll will total 7.

Eighter from Decatur: wagering that the next roll will total 8.

Front line: craps lingo for the pass line.

Front-line winner: wagering that the next roll will be a 7.

Hardways bet: betting that numbers 4, 6, 8, and 10 will be rolled as pairs—two 2s, two 3s, two4, and two 5s respectively—before a 7 or your number rolled not as a pair. Hard eight in craps is double 4s, hard 6 is double 3s, hard 10 is double 5s, etc.

Hot hand: this shooter is hot—connecting with points and numbers.

Hot roll: another term for a hot shooter.

Hot table: the action at this table is red-hot.

Jimmie Hick: number 6.

Line away: wagering that the next roll will be a 7.

Little Joe from Kokomo: wagering that the next roll will be a 4.

Long and strong: Got to hit that backboard if you want it to count.

Midnight: lingo for the number 12 or wagering that the next roll will be a 12.

Nina from Pasadena: wagering that the next roll will total 9.

Outstanding in your field: wagering that the next roll will total 12.

Pair of aces in the wrong places: number 2.

Puppy paws: wagering that the next roll will total 10.

Quarters: lingo for $25 chips.

Six ace: wagering that the next roll will be a 7.

Six five, no jive: wagering that the next roll will total 11.

Six one, you're all done: wagering that the next roll will be a 7.

Snake eyes: lingo for the number 2 or wagering that the next roll will be a 2.

Square pair: wagering that the next roll will be a Hard 8 (two 4s).

Thirty-two juice roll: wagering that the next roll will be a 5.

Two aces: number 2.

Two rolls and no coffee: lingo for two rolls, then a seven out.

Up pops the devil: wagering that the next roll will be a 7.

Winner on the dark side: wagering that the next roll will be a 3.

Yo: number 11.
Yo eleven: wagering that the next roll will total 11.

Before ending our discussion of craps, let's go back for a moment to the come-out roll, where the odds favor the right bettor. The probability on a pass-line bet is that a 7 can be rolled six ways and an 11 two ways, for a total of eight ways.

But a craps, or a don't-pass, bet can be rolled only on a 2 or 3, with a total of three ways. Then there's the 12, which can be rolled only one way. But a push, or standoff, doesn't really count. So you see, a natural has the greater probability.

I hope I have served up enough information to persuade you to diversify your gambling . . . and definitely consider the game of craps.

But if the roar and congestion around a craps table gets to you, you might consider moving on to the baccarat table, which has the reputation, justified or not, for being the most elegant and refined of the casino games.

Big Bucks from Baccarat
and European Games, Too
9

In movies and novels, baccarat is presented as an expensive game, out of reach for the budget gambler. Well, I will show you that this table game is affordable, especially when you play the mini-version at a mini-price.

Baccarat is trying to shake its blue-blood image.

In reality, it's an excellent card game for the low-limit novice, because it requires no skill and little knowledge. And the house edge is under 1.5 percent.

If you like blackjack, you'll probably like baccarat, because the two games are similar. Baccarat was invented first and, unlike blackjack, it does not require extensive strategy. All you really have to do is pick a side: banker or player. I can see the growing popularity of such a simple and fast game with fixed rules and easy decisions.

However, I know firsthand how easy it is to feel intimidated by baccarat. The table is usually in a secluded pit area with rich decor and tuxedo-clad people everywhere.

For a long time I wouldn't even get close enough to find out the rules or what was going on in those plush areas. Now I know what I was missing . . . a lot!

Baccarat is a card game that is dealt from a device called a shoe. Some tables can accommodate 16 players, though number 13 is always skipped.

The shoe holds six to eight decks of cards.

In each game, the player and the banker are each dealt a hand of two cards.

You bet on either of the two hands to win.

Winning means coming closest to a value of 9, without going over.

Directly in front of you are two boxes. The box closer to you is for betting that the player will win the next hand, and the box farther from you is for betting that the banker will win. Two dealers are responsible for paying and removing bets. Each dealer works one end of the table.

All number cards, 2 through 9, count as their face value, or the number of pips on the card. All 10s and face cards count as 10. Aces count as 1.

No hand can be worth more than 9. If it is, the last digit of the total is used.

For example, if the hand has a king (10) and a 2, then it totals not 12 but 2.

In other words, to quickly determine the value of a hand greater than 9, simply use the last digit of the total number, such as 9 for 19, 0 for 20, or 7 for 17.

It's important to remember that no hand is too bad or too good to win, because the count can change with the third card, if one is required. This creates a mounting suspense, and that's what makes baccarat such an exciting adventure.

The casino encourages players to deal cards from the shoe, but you are not obligated to deal. The shoe passes around the table in a counterclockwise direction.

The player holding the shoe is considered the banker. However, the banker does not take any additional risk. Technically, he or she is not the banker, but merely represents the banker's hand.

The dealer will determine which player has the largest bet on the player's hand, and will give that person the two cards representing the player's hand.

Both hands are displayed, and the totals for each hand are called out.

At this point, the game may or may not be over, depending on whether or not a third card is required. The dealer instructs the banker when to draw a third card, in accordance with the game's strict rules. The maximum number of cards in any hand is three.

Third-card rules are as follows:

PLAYER: Dealt a total of 1, 2, 3, 4, 5, or 10: draws a card. Dealt 6 or 7: stands. Dealt 8 or 9: natural. Banker cannot draw.

BANKER: 5 or less: draws; 6 or more: stands if the player does not draw a third card. If the player draws a third card, the banker dealt 2 must draw. Dealt 3: draws to player 1, 2, 3, 4, 5, 6, 7, 9, or 10, does not draw to player 8. Dealt 4: draws to player 2, 3, 4, 5, 6, or 7, does not draw to 1, 8, 9, or 10. Dealt 5: draws to player 4, 5, 6, 7, does not draw to 1, 2, 3, 8, 9, or 10. Dealt 6: draws to player 6 or 7, does not draw to 1, 2, 3, 4, 5, 8, 9, 10. Dealt 7: stands. Dealt 8 or 9—natural; player cannot draw.

Card Counting Basics

Cards more favorable to the bank hand: 9, 8, 10, J, Q, and K in order of strength; 4, 3, 2, and 5 are player-favorable cards. Ace, 6, and 8 are neutral—no favor to either hand.

Baccarat can progress as quickly as five hands per minute. The average shoe will deal about 82 hands, of which the bank will win 38, the player 36, with 8 ties (about every tenth hand). The shoe almost always favors the casino and is used to reduce the casino advantage over the player.

Bank hands win more because the bank stands on a 7, 8, or 9, whereas a player stands on 6, 7, 8, or 9; the bank can draw on a 6, but a player cannot. There's the rub. After the third card is dealt, if required, the dealer announces the winner (saying, for example, "Banker wins 5 over 3").

Mathematically, the banker's hand has a slight edge over the player's hand, because of the third-card rules. This would mean that you should always bet on the banker's hand. However, the casinos have come up with a neat solution to this. They charge players a 5 percent commission each time they bet on the banker to win. The dealers are responsible for keeping track of how much commission is owed. In front of each dealer is a row of numbered boxes; each time you have a commission payable, it is noted at your corresponding box number with token chips. Before you are finished playing, make sure you have enough money in front of you to cover this debt.

Besides betting that the player or banker will win, you could bet that there will be a tie. But with a casino advantage of 14 percent, the tie bet is the only bad bet in baccarat. A tie is always a push, so the banker or player bets stand when a tie is dealt.

Most casinos will provide a score sheet and pen upon request. You can use these to track trends, patterns, and streaks in the making. Make columns headed "Banker" and "Player," and mark down each winning total. Strike a line through the box for a tie. Circle the hands that you win.

In baccarat, unlike blackjack, you can sit out or skip hands; just tell the dealer "No bet." The break time can be used to analyze your scorecard and strategize your next move. Some gamblers keep these scorecards for a running history of their play.

Now, about that mini-version model of baccarat.

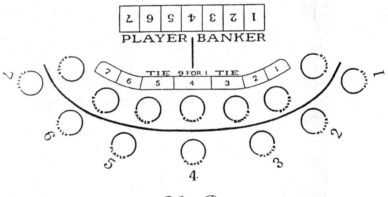

Mini Bac

I strongly suggest that you "test-drive" a mini-baccarat table, especially if you are a low-limit or novice player. The only difference between mini-baccarat and the full-size version of the game is that in mini-baccarat, all hands are dealt by a dealer, not the players.

A few years ago, in Laughlin, the only mini-baccarat table I saw was at Harrah's, out on the floor, and it was obviously very new. After each hand, the dealers had to check their charts for third-card rules. There were six players—the table's limit—and we had great fun helping the dealers count the hands. No intimidation here! Everyone was getting an education. When you approach a mini-baccarat table, note the posted minimum bet and commission. The Harrah's mini-baccarat table minimum bet was $5, with a 25-cent commission when the banker's hand won.

The road to profits in baccarat is definitely with progressive betting after each win. The only baccarat strategy I recommend is to bet on the hand that won the last game, because streaks are legendary in this game. A banker or player can win ten, fifteen, or even twenty hands in a row after the shoe opens up, so give this strategy a try.

European Variations: Basic Terms and Rules

Punto banco closely resembles American baccarat, but much of the terminology involved is different. For example, the shoe is called the sabot, the player is the punter, and the dealer is the croupier (here, the croupier runs the game).

The tie bet pays eight times the stake and may not be more than a quarter of the maximum stake. The first card brought out by the croupier and turned over determines the number of cards discarded before the first game of a new shoe begins. If the first card is a face card, 10 unturned cards are discarded; if a 7 shows, seven unturned cards are discarded, and so on.

This all makes card counting a little more difficult.

All cards are dealt faceup.

In chemin de fer, you cannot bet on the banker or the player. You must be one or the other, and the casino has no direct involvement. Bettors wager among themselves, and the house takes a commission.

The player who acts as the banker, by making the largest bid, retains possession of the shoe. He or she places the bet or bid (currency) in the middle of the table, and is responsible for covering all losing bets, collecting all winning bank bets while betting the banker's hand. The other players can now bet against all (the bank, or banco) or any portion of this money. The highest bidder is then dealt the player's hand.

93

There is no tie bet in this game, and no money changes hands when there is a tie.

The casino takes a 5 percent commission, or rake, as in poker, on all winning bank hands. In return, the casino provides a croupier as referee, a table, and any necessary equipment.

Third-card rules are different; bank hand totals of 3 and 5 offer draw or stand options, and your bankroll requirement, if you want to play banker, is higher.

In baccarat à deux tableaux (double-table baccarat), the dealer, or croupier, acts as the banker, deals all the cards, and banks all bets. The dealer stands between two tables joined in the middle and deals two player's hands, one hand to each table, then two cards for banker's hands.

Players always bet on a player's hand, which pays even money; or they can bet on both tables by placing a bet on the line dividing the two tables. The rules are the same as those for chemin de fer.

This game is usually privately run, with a cut going to the casino. This is not the best baccarat bet, as the person making the most money is the one who puts up the bankroll.

Trente et quarante, or 30/40, is a simple French card game. Also called rouge et noir (red and black), it is played with six decks of cards and offers four bets: rouge, noir, couleur and inverse.

All are paid off at even money. Aces are worth 1, face or court cards, 10; all others are taken at face value.

Two hands are dealt. Each row must exceed 30, but not 40. The first row of cards is black, the second red, and whichever hand is lower or closer to 30 wins. If the first card dealt in the first row is the same color as in the winning row, the color bet wins; if first card is of the opposite color, the inverse bet wins.

A tie is a push. However, if both rows equal 31, then bets lose only half the value. Players may then divide their bet or wait for the next deal. The bet will be free if it wins.

All of these games have a reputation for European flair, but the one that epitomizes continental elegance is roulette, whose revolving wheel we will visit next.

Roulette Strategies for Spinning Profits

10

I can't walk by a roulette wheel without stopping to watch the players and the action.

What an exciting game!

But the grim fact is that a double-zero roulette wheel has a 5.26 percent house advantage. When the wheel has only a single-zero slot, the house edge is cut in half, down to odds acceptable to an educated gambler.

The casino's 5.26 percent advantage is calculated based on the single-number bet that pays only 35-1, instead of the "true odds," or full pay, of 37-1. In other words, the payoff is $2 short on a winning $1 bet.

So, $2 divided by 38 equals 5.26 percent. The single-zero wheel is $1 short; $1 divided by 38 equals 2.63 percent.

The five-number bet of 0, 00, 1, 2, and 3 blasts that 5.26 percent out of the house with an edge of 7.89 percent. Just don't do it!

In roulette, outside bets are placed in the boxes and columns on the outer areas of the layout. Inside bets are placed directly on a number or on a line between numbers, known as "streets." Below is a summary of bets that can be placed, along with the payouts:

Bets and Payouts

A. Straight up—any one number, including 0 and 00: 35 to 1
B. Column—any twelve numbers in a column: 2 to 1

C.   Dozen—the first twelve, second twelve or third twelve: 2 to 1

D.   Red or black:1 to 1

E.   Odd or even:1 to 1

F.   1 to 18 or 19 to 36:1 to 1

G.   Split—any two neighboring numbers:17 to 1

H.   Row—any three numbers in a row: 11 to 1

I.   Corner—any of the four contiguous numbers: 8 to 1

J.   Five numbers—0, 00, 1, 2, and 3: 6 to 1 Don't do it!

K.   Double row—any six numbers in two rows: 5 to 1

European roulette wheels have only a single zero, positioned between black 26 and red 32. This type of wheel, the best one to play, reduces the casino advantage to an acceptable 2.63 percent.

Another advantage is the en prison, or surrender, rule on even-money bets. When the 0 comes up, your bet remains or is captured for the next spin.

If you win on the next spin, you don't get paid for the win, but you are allowed to take your original bet back; in effect, you lose only half your bet. The house edge on even-money bets with the en prison ("captured") rule is reduced to 1.35 percent.

Now you know why roulette is the most popular game in Europe. You will also find this "captured" rule at Atlantic City casinos. As of this writing, Monte Carlo, Fiesta Henderson, Paris, MGM Grand, and Stratosphere in Vegas offer the single-zero wheel. In Canada, the Montreal casino has single-zero roulette tables as well.

But beware! These roulette games will have higher minimum bets for this preferred option.

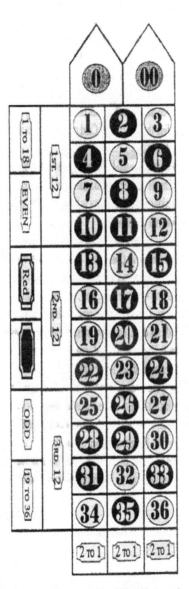

Place Red or Black bet on outside middle table as per layout.
Black Bet covers all eighteen black number-also bet Column 3
-under #36 for eight red numbers.
Red Bet covers all eighteen red numbers- also bet Column 2
-under #35 for eight black numbers.

99

Below are five roulette systems that I recommend. The intelligent player will make a series of predetermined bets rather than betting all over the table.

1) After observing for a while, I will bet the minimum on, let's say, black, and then place an additional minimum bet on the third column of numbers below the number 36.

   This bet covers all eighteen black numbers, and the third column has the most red numbers on the layout (eight). Therefore, I'm covering a total of twenty-six numbers. On a win, I get even money on the black or 2 to 1 on the column. Better still, I can win on both bets if my black number is in the third column after the final spin.

   I can reverse this minimum wager and bet on all eighteen red numbers, with an additional bet at the bottom of the middle column under 35 to cover eight black numbers. Again, I have covered twenty-six numbers.

   I have had good success with this method. After six wins in a row at one Vegas roulette table, I taught the whole table the system and drove the croupier nuts.

2) I call this one the dozen/column betting strategy. If you place four bets, two dozen, and two column, you will cover all numbers except four inside and both the single and the double zeros; therefore, thirty-two numbers will be covered, with some numbers duplicated. All wins pay 2-1.

   For example: 1-12 is the first dozen, 13-24, the second dozen. The second column, under 35 and the third column, under 36, are also covered. You can mix and match—say, with the third dozen bet and the first column bet under 34; always bet two dozens and two columns on each spin.

3) Five-number-combinations strategy involves betting the first chip on a six-number combination, then placing a straight-up bet on four other numbers, thereby covering ten numbers for each spin. Here are some sample bets using six-number combos and four numbers straight up:

1–6: 20, 26, 8, 10
4–9: 13, 14, 15, 10
10–15: 16, 17, 18, 28
13–18: 11, 12, 27, 28
19–24: 1, 2, 4, 26
28–33: 00, 22, 24, 35
31–36: 0, 00, 29, 30

4) Nine-number combination strategy involves nine split bets straddling two numbers to cover a total of eighteen numbers for each spin. Split your bet on: 1 and 4, 2 and 5, 3 and 6, 11 and 12, 26 and 27, 25 and 28, 31 and 34, 32 and 35, 33 and 36.

5) Twelve-number combination strategy involves twelve split bets straddling two numbers to cover a total of eighteen numbers, or half the layout, excluding the double zeros, for each spin. Each winning bet pays 17-1.

You can place your twelve split bets in many different series on the layout, utilizing two twin-split wagers on the three numbers that run across the layout, known as a "street."

For example, the numbers 1-2-3 are a street. You can place a split bet between 1 and 2 and another split bet between 2 and 3, then place split bets on 4 and 5 and 5 and 6, continuing down six streets.

If you are standing at the bottom of the roulette table looking up from the 34, 35, 36 end, this strategy combination will look like a ladder with six split bets straddling the first and second columns and six bets covering the second and third columns.

Place your twelve bets at the top of the layout to cover numbers 1-18, or choose the bottom of the layout to cover numbers 19-36.

Or six chips at the top of the layout over 1-9 and bottom six chips at the bottom for 28-36.

Or four chips in each dozen area of the layout—two split bets on the 4, 5, 6 street, plus two on the 7, 8, 9 street will get you a dozen. Mix and match, but in a consistent fashion when placing these twelve bets.

Now you have five roulette strategies to keep you busy while you are looking for that single-zero roulette wheel, where your best chances for profit await. Keep spinning those wheels, and don't forget about progressive betting, pressing, and upping your bet after each win.

On now to pai gow poker, another card game in which the house has an acceptably low advantage.

Bank on Pai Gow Poker

11

Pai gow poker is included in the top ten because of the low 2.5 percent casino advantage.

The difference between pai gow and pai gow poker is that pai gow is an Asian game played with thirty-two dominoes, a brass holder, and dice. Pai gow poker, on the other hand, is an American derivative played with standard playing cards. In both games, players are required to set two hands, a high and a low. These hands compete against the banker's two hands.

The cards in pai gow poker are ranked as in standard poker hands, the exception being that the deck contains a joker, which can be played as an ace or a high card to finish a straight, flush, straight flush, or royal flush. The basics are as follows:

- You must win both hands to win your bet. All players play against the banker, which can be the dealer or a player putting up the required funds.
- Each player receives seven cards and must make two poker hands: the high hand, made up of five cards, and the low hand, containing two cards.
- The highest five-card hand is five aces, and the highest two-card hand is two aces.

A pai gow poker table has six players' seats and a dealer, like a blackjack table. The player's high hand is displayed closest to the space in front of them, while low two-card hand is placed on top of the high hand, toward the dealer.

A chung, or marker, is set in front of the banker.

The game's rotation is counterclockwise. The dealer shuffles and deals seven hands of seven cards facedown, which equals forty-nine cards, leaving four in the deck.

Standard **PAI GOW** Poker Table

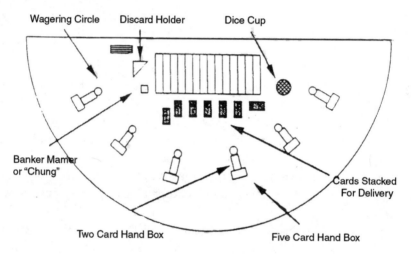

The receiver of the first hand is determined by a throw from a cup containing three dice. After the players receive their seven cards facedown, they must form two hands. As mentioned, the rank of the five-card high hand must be higher than that of the two-card low hand. Any player's hand that is set incorrectly automatically loses.

Most casino dealers will assist in this placement if requested, and the dealer sets the bank hand according to fixed house rules. Once all hands are set, the dealer will compare the players' hands rank with the banker's hand to determine the payouts.

- If one of your hands is higher in rank than the dealer's and the other is lower, the result is a tie (this happens approximately 45 percent of the time) and your bet remains on the layout. If the banker bests both of your hands, you lose your wager.
- If both hands are identical (known as a copy), the banker wins.
- A win pays even money, less a 5 percent commission paid immediately.

Casinos have different rules as to how many times a player can act as banker. The dealer will ask each player in turn if they wish to be the banker; the same player cannot bank two consecutive hands. If the casino allows you to be banker every second or third hand, this is definitely to your advantage. Note, however, that the banker must have sufficient chips to cover all of the other players' wagers.

Pai gow poker rankings are as follows: Five aces (four aces plus joker); royal flush; A-2-3-4-5 (this is usually the second-highest straight flush, but not all casinos and card rooms follow this rule—check before you play); all other straight flushes; four of a kind; full house; flush; straight; three of a kind; two pair; one pair; and high card.

Strategy tips for pai gow poker

- No pairs: Play the second and third highest-ranked cards as the low hand and the remaining five cards as high hand (e.g., dealt K, Q, 10, 8, 6, 5, 2). Set the Q, 10 as low hand and K, 8, 6, 5, 2 as high hand.
- One pair: The pair is set in the high hand and your next two highest-ranked ards as low hand.
- Two pair: Depends on the rank of the pairs. If one of your pairs is aces, kings, or queens, then split the pairs, putting the As, Ks or Qs in your high hand and the other pair as low hand. For all other pairs, play them as two pair in the high hand and a king or ace in your low hand. If you were not dealt a king or an ace for the low hand, then you are safer to split the pairs, with the high pair in your high hand and the low pair in your low hand.
- Three pair: The highest-ranking pair should be your low hand.
- Three of a kind: Split three aces or kings, playing one ace or king

in the low hand and the pair in the high hand. All other three of a kind arrangements should be played in the high hand, with the two highest cards used as the low hand.

• Straights and flushes: These should be your high hand, with the two remaining cards used as your low hand. These two rankings are easy to overlook, so check for these two hands first before developing a low-hand strategy.

• Full house: Use the three of a kind in the high hand and the high pair as the low hand—this is by far the most effective split in this situation.

• Four of a kind: Always split four aces, kings, and queens. Play one pair as your low hand and the other in your high hand. With four Jacks through 7s, play them as a four of a kind in your high hand only if you have at least a queen that you can use in your low hand. If you don't have the latter, then split the four of a kind (two in your low hand, two in your high hand). With four 2s through 6s, never split. Always play them in your high hand.

• Five aces: Split the aces and play a pair of aces in your low hand and three aces in your high hand.

• The casino's advantage is about 2.8 percent, lowered to 2.5 percent with perfect strategy.

• A skillful banker can play an even game against the casino; therefore, try for the banker position often, placing larger bets as your wagering plan allows.

• Bet the minimum only when you have to be the player.

If you enjoy pai gow poker, and like forming poker hands, you might want to try other forms of poker, in which skill plays a greater role.

These days, casinos often have poker rooms, with wagering for every budget.

Four Poker Games— It's in the Cards

12

Three of the most popular games dealt in poker rooms today are Seven-Card Stud, Texas Hold 'Em, and Omaha (Hi and Hi-Lo). These games differ greatly from most casino games in that players compete against one another in games in which skill, "reading" your opponent, and "bluffing" (betting with a poor hand) play a far greater role.

This chapter discusses the basic rules for Limit Seven-Card Stud, Texas Hold 'Em, Omaha, and Three-Card Poker, and provides some general strategic guidelines for each. (Limit poker differs from other forms of wagering, such as pot limit and no limit, in that there are limits placed on how much can be bet at any point in the hand.) Some poker lingo is provided after the Hold 'Em section.

But first some important general information and advice about playing live poker in casinos:

- The hierarchy of poker hands is: royal flush, straight flush, four of a kind, full house, flush, straight, three of a kind, two pair, one pair, to less than a pair.
- Poker players bet against one another and not against the house.
- It is advisable to check the table postings for betting limits and to ask what the rake is (the percentage the house takes for providing a dealer and tables). It is usually 5 percent or a maximum dollar amount that is a flat fee or hourly rate.
- Generally, your buy-in should be ten to twenty times the top bet.

- I recommend that you set a stop-loss limit and a win goal. If you run out of chips and go "all-in," you'll be allowed to finish the hand; however, you are excluded from betting in the remaining rounds. If there is further betting, it goes into a side pot. You can only win the amount from each other player that you have put into the pot. Whatever extra is bet into the pot will go to the highest-ranking hand held by a player who finishes the hand.
- I recommend that novice poker players start with the low-limit tables in the casino's poker room. When you can beat (win consistently) at that level, you are ready to move up to higher-limit tables.
- Observe before jumping in, or take advantage of the free lessons offered by most casinos.
- Contact the poker-room manager, and if a seat is not available for your requested game, you can be put on a waiting list and paged.
- Many newbie poker players prefer the comfort of online poker because you can play on them for free, and the poker forums provide valuable information. There is also abundant poker software, which can help beginners sharpen their skills.
- In any given situation, a player has four basic options: 1) bet; 2) pass—to check or drop out instead of betting—or check—pass with out betting but remain in the game; 3) call and bet—the same as the previous bet; or 4) raise the bet—often there's a limit of three raise bets in any round.
- Checking and then raising ("check-raising") is usually allowed.
- A "button" moves around the table clockwise to indicate the dealer's position.

Seven-Card Stud

Rules:

- Each player places the ante, or forced opening bet, into the pot before the hand begins.
- The cards are dealt one at a time to each player.
- Each player will receive two cards facedown, then four cards faceup,

108

followed by a final card which is dealt facedown.

- After every player receives the initial two facedown cards and one faceup card, the first round of betting occurs, known as Third Street.
- The player with the lowest card showing starts the betting. This forced bet known as the "bring-in" bet. If two (or more) players have the same low card, then the card suit determines who bets first, in this order: clubs, diamonds, hearts, and spades.
- Each player in turn (moving clockwise) must then either call (equal the bet), raise the bet, or fold.
- When the betting is completed, the dealer deals another round of cards faceup to each player, known as Fourth Street. This time the player with the highest hand showing bets first, and all other players must "act" (call, check, or raise) in order.
- This sequence of betting continues, with Fifth Street and Sixth Street. When a pair shows, or it's at least Fifth Street, a player can usually bet the high limit, as posted. (Generally, the high limit is double the low limit.)
- The last card, Seventh Street, is dealt facedown ("down and dirty"). A final round of betting occurs, followed by the showdown, or revealing of the hands.
- The highest hand wins the pot.

Texas Hold 'Em

Rules:

- The main difference between this game and Seven-Card Stud is that this one involves community cards, or cards that all players in the game use to complete their hands. Eventually, each player will have seven cards, two of their own (hidden) and five community cards (visible).
- The casino dealer deals out two cards, facedown, one at a time, to each player.
- The first player to receive a card is the player to the left of the button.

This position is called the "small blind," and the player must ante half the amount of the big blind.

- The second player to receive a card is called the "big blind," and this player must ante the full "bring-in" bet. For instance, on a $1–2 table, the small blind would ante $1 and the big blind $2.
- After all players receive their two cards, the first player to "act" (decide on an action) can call (match the amount anted by the big blind), raise, or fold. Checking is not allowed on this round. Players, in turn, must match the big blind or, if the blind is raised, match the raise.
- The dealer now deals three cards faceup in the center of the table. These are called "the flop," and a round of betting begins. (Of course, if all players check here, no further money will be added to the pot.)
- The dealer places a fourth card faceup on the table, again followed by a betting round. This part of the hand is called "Fourth Street" or "the turn," and the bet is usually double what it was after the flop.
- The fifth and final card (called "the river") is placed by the dealer faceup in the middle of the table, and this is the final round of betting. As with the turn, the river bet is generally double the amount of the big blind (ante).
- Each player chooses their best five-card hand among the seven cards—the two cards dealt facedown at the beginning of the game and the five community cards in the middle of the layout.
- The winning hand is the highest poker hand.

Lingo for Texas Hold 'Em (and Omaha Games)

Blind (small blind, big blind): Forced bets that take the place of an ante. The person to the left of the dealer pays the small blind, and the person after that pays the big blind. After the flop, the small blind acts first and the big blind acts second for the remainder of the hand.

Community or board cards: Cards in the middle of the table that are shared by all players.

The flop: The first three faceup cards in Texas Hold 'Em.

The turn: The fourth community (or board) card in Texas Hold 'Em. Also known as Fourth Street.

The river: The fifth and final faceup card in Texas Hold 'Em, after the turn.

Position: The order in which the players act. To have "position" on a player means to act after them.

The button: The best position is held by the person who bets last, called the button, because from this position one can survey the other players before making a decision. Therefore, the person who act first (the small blind) is in the worst position.

Omaha

Omaha Hi and Omaha Hi-Lo Split are the two versions of this poker game, which, like Texas Hold 'Em and unlike Seven-Card Stud, uses community cards. Omaha Hi-Lo Split is also known as Omaha Hi-Lo, Omaha Eight or Better, and Omaha Eight. It is a game in which the high and the low hands split the pot, unless there is no qualifying low hand or one player "scoops" the pot (wins both high and low hands). The name "Omaha" refers to the high hand only. The streets and the betting schemes for limit forms of Omaha are identical to those in Texas Hold 'Em.

The difference between both versions of Omaha and Texas Hold 'Em is that with Omaha the player is dealt four starting cards, not two. It is mandatory that each player must use two cards from their hand and three cards from the community board. Using three cards instead of two from their hand to form the best hand can confuse a new player who is used to Hold 'Em Play. It takes time to learn to read the many combinations that result from being dealt four cards. Hand values for Omaha Hi are generally much stronger than in Texas Hold 'Em.

In Omaha Hi-Lo, also called Omaha Eight or Better, to qualify for a low hand, there must be no cards higher than 8 in your five-card hand. Therefore, since you're using two cards from your hand, there must be three cards on the board that are 8 or lower. If there is no low hand as described, the player with the highest hand wins.

Additional Poker Terms

Stud Poker

Ante: A small bet placed before receiving your hand. The ante is not part of a call made with the first bet, and if you fold, the ante bet is lost.

Blank: A card of no help to your current hand.

Bring in: Once all the cards are dealt, the lowest card on the table must make a small bet, of approximately one-third the size of the lower limit set, and cannot fold. For example, for a $10/$20 stake, the player must bet at least $3. If another player raises to $10, the bring-in player has three options: a) fold, b) call the additional $7, or c) raise to $20.

Door card: First up card dealt in a round of Stud Poker.

Fifth Street: This is your third up card received. At this juncture in the game, the betting limits double and some players fold.

Hole cards: Cards known only to the player, and therefore held "in the hole."

Pocket pair: A pair in the hole; the term is used for both Stud and Hold 'Em.

Rag(s): Weak card(s).

Trips: Three of a kind, or triples.

Turn: Your fourth card received.

Texas Hold 'Em

All-in: Betting your available bankroll at one time, especially powerful in a no-limit game.

Bad beat: You take a bad beat when an opponent draws out on you. See "draw out."

Big slick: An ace or king in the hold—a great starting hand. There are several possibilities from this hand including high pair and/or high straight.

Broadway: A-K-Q-J-10, the highest straight.

Button: The last player to bet. This is an advantage in that you have the opportunity to watch the other players before making a decision.

Calling station: A player who calls many bets but rarely bets or raises.

Cover: One player's available bankroll can cover another player's all-in bet.

Draw out: To be behind in the hand and catch a winning hand in a later street.

Fill up: To complete a full house.

Fishy: A weak player.

Gutshot: One draw that completes an inside straight. For example, an 8 completing a hand of 6-7-9-10.

Heads-up: Two players competing for one pot.

Hit with the deck: Excellent cards coming your way for quite a while. 'Tis a very good thing.

Muck: The name of the discard pile in poker. You hand is officially dead when it hits the muck. To throw away your cards is often called "mucking" them.

Nuts: The best possible hand, given the board.

Overcard: A card that is higher than the highest cards on board.

Rainbow: A flop that displays three different suits, making a flush unlikely (it would now require two running, or consecutive, cards).

Rake: A percentage and/or flat fee deducted from the pot after each betting round, for the casino services. These services include a dealer and equipment.

Rock: A player who plays only strong hands and calls few bets; also known as a "tight" player.

Spike: To snag a needed card.

Washing the cards: The dealer blends the deck of cards in a circular motion with both hands to perform a shuffle.

Omaha Hi-Lo Poker

Baby: A low card, generally a 5 or lower; offers the possibility of making a perfect low.

Banana: A card between 9 and a king; same as a brick.

Brick: The term for a card between 9 and a king, as it is unlikely to qualify for an 8 low.

Escape: You have just snagged a card that will likely win half the pot.

Free roll: A nice position. You are guaranteed the high or low, plus the possibly of winning the other half.

Quartered: A split between two players with equivalent hands for half of half of the pot.

Runners: Two cards dealt in consecutive rounds that make a winning hand.

Scoop: You have just won the whole pot in a hi-lo game—congratulations!

Wheel: A hand containing A-2-3-4-5 is termed a wheel because it counts as a perfect low and a 5-high straight. A steel wheel is when all of the cards are suited, or in the same suit.

Poker Strategy

In Seven-Card Stud, since many cards are dealt faceup, it's crucial to keep track of all the cards that have been visible, especially those that have been folded. This will give you valuable information about what your opponents might hold "in the hole" (their facedown cards). It also gives you information on the likelihood of making your own hand.

In all forms of live poker, it's important as well to pay close attention to your opponents' body language and facial expressions. This is called "reading" your opponent. You need to study all of your opponents' betting patterns. Unlike other casino games, poker has a large human element. You do not need the best hand to win, and bluffing plays a significant role.

In general, you can minimize your losses by not staying in pots too long ("chasing"). You cannot make every hand a winner, and there is no shame in being bluffed out of a hand. Those who bluff too often eventually get caught, or "called down." Intelligent players know when to fold 'em ("lay down") and when to press the action.

In Seven-Card Stud, it's best to fold on Third Street unless you have at least a pair; if the pair is low, you should also have an ace, king, or queen kicker.

If you don't improve your three-card flush or straight by the fourth card, fold. Here it's especially important to be aware of how many of the cards needed for your straight or flush are already on the board.

If another player has a higher pair than yours, fold unless you also have an odd card higher in rank than that high pair.

In Texas Hold 'Em, it's generally good strategy to play strong starting cards ("premium hands"), such as A-A, K-K, Q-Q, J-J, or A-K, A-Q. Hand strengths usually go up, depending on how many people are in the hand and on your betting position.

In general:

- Fold if you have a pair lower than 7s.
- You should look for lower cards in the flop than the rank of your pair.
- When you have the best possible hand (the "nuts") you should try to keep as many players in the pot for as long as possible.
- When you have a strong hand it's best to play aggressively, raising and getting rid of players' hands with good drawing possibilities (players looking to complete a straight or a flush, in particular).
- If you feel that your hand has become second best, fold.
- Marginal or drawing hands should be played as cheaply as possible, either by checking or by making nominal bets.

In Omaha, you may believe that you have eight two-card combinations with the four cards in hand; however, there are actually only six.

While many Hold 'Em players are showing great interest in Omaha, they should not fall into the trap of utilizing the same strategy for both games.

Unlike Texas Hold 'Em, where strong starting cards occur if the first two cards are two aces, two kings, two queens, or A-K or A-Q suited, you will have to be cautious to work with not only the flop but other players' hands to come out ahead. In Omaha, you'll need much stronger hands after the flop to continue, and many players will stick around for the later streets with flush or straight draws. The game can be costly, so check your bankroll before participating.

A final word on bluffing: Pick your times and your players.

It's easier to bluff against one player and easier against good players, who respect the odds and the art of poker, as opposed to weak players who stay in the pot forever.

Three-Card Poker

This is also an excellent choice now found in many casinos.

There are three betting circles in front of each player titled "Pair Plus," "Ante," and "Play."

You place your ante and play bets first.

The pair plus bet is a player option that pays for a pair or better.

You develop the best hand possible from the three cards dealt. For example, a 7-8-9 unsuited is a straight; if all of the cards were suited, you would hold a straight flush. Three nonconsecutive suited cards is a flush (for example, 2-7-K). Therefore, a straight beats a flush in this game.

The dealer must have a queen or higher for the game to proceed. If not, your bet is a push, or a draw.

In poker, a bad streak or a series of bad decisions can seriously dent your bankroll. On our next stop, bingo, the risk is limited at the outset, but the fun and the potential winnings are not!

Bingo!

13

The game of bingo has always been a best bet simply because, except in progressive games, there is always a winner, unlike with a lottery.

It is estimated that in the United States two million people play bingo every day. Indian casinos are in the bingo business big-time, and many have separate bingo halls. Plus, bingo played for charity has been around forever. Casinos are not charities, but today they offer varieties of bingo. Often in a restaurant in a casino, one can follow along on a TV monitor!

The good news for bingo lovers in Vegas is that Nevada casinos actually run bingo games at a loss to bring in casino gamblers. If you play during slow hours at any bingo hall, you will increase your odds for a big payout, especially for progressive games. (In progressive bingo, the jackpot prize builds daily, weekly, or monthly. If there is no winner in x number of calls, the jackpot and number of bingo calls increases for the next time.)

The bad news for bingo players is that playing multiple cards increases your chances only slightly. You have to consider the total number of cards being played for that regular game (not progressives; we'll talk about that later). Let's say there are 3,000 cards in play. There is only 1 predetermined payout, although more than one winner can split the pot, so 1 out of 3,000 cards wins. With 5 cards the increase is only 5 in 3,000, instead of 1 in 3,000—not very much.

The win possibilities in progressive games are as follows: with 50 numbers, 1 in 212,086; but it gets better for 55 or fewer numbers at 1 in 10,359.

My own bingo career got off to a rocky start. Maybe this story can save you some embarrassment.

Once, years back, I was enjoying a girls night out with five friends, all of whom were much more experienced at bingo than the only amateur, yours truly.

My past experience had been with my harried mother, who had tried to keep four children occupied by having us play bingo for candies. So I had seen a card before and figured I was qualified for the big time.

When we entered the huge, crowded bingo hall, I felt winning prospects in the air. There I sat, in the very first game, with my two little cards, chips in the air ready to cover those numbers. It was just a matter of time before I hit, I figured.

And sure enough, after approximately twenty numbers were called, what a thrill—I found myself screaming "BINGO!" at the top of my lungs. My friends were awestruck at this amazing beginner's luck; they sat stunned as the verifier approached.

I had one line filled, a winner, I thought—until I was quietly told that in this particular game you had to fill your entire card to win.

Can you imagine how red my face was?

Two of my friends were mortified, because they expected to return to this same bingo hall soon. The other three laughed until tears rolled.

"You see," I tried to explain, "when I played with my brother and sisters, one line was a winner."

I tried blaming my mother, but that isn't fair. She had been trying to make sure that the games were short, and that hopefully each of us won at least once. My mother's sense of fairness has always been one of her biggest assets.

Even after that experience, however, I have returned to this game often, and with great pleasure. But since then I have always listened to the rules more carefully. And you should too!

A Condensed History of Bingo

Like many casino games today, bingo's history can be traced back to Europe. Information about the game was first recorded in Italy in the 1500s.

The French added a deck of cards in the late 1700s and the name "lotto." The British military bestowed the names "house" or "housy-housy" in the 1800s. At about the same time, a form of bingo called "kino" or "keno" was making its way into the American culture. The Great Depression saw a surge in the popularity of bingo, or "screeno," as it was known when played in movie houses. Moviegoers received bingo cards for the price of admission, vying for cash prizes. Of course, the game of keno has evolved today as a popular casino game and is played much the same as bingo.

Other variations of the American game are fortune, lucky, radio, and beano. Beano appeared destined to be the name that stuck, but in 1929 a salesman from New York observed the game at a local carnival. While he was playing with his friends, a slip of the tongue from a startled winner resulted in the name Bingo.

Bingo Basics

- Bingo cards resemble a five-by-five grid with twenty-five correspon-ding numbers filling the boxes under the five letters B-I-N-G-O.
- The middle space is marked FREE in most games, under the letter N.
- The numbers on bingo cards are a selection from 1 to 75. (British bingo cards use 1 through 90.)
- Each number appears only once on any bingo card.

There are fifteen number possibilities under each letter of the word BIN-GO. Under B, the numbers run from B1 through B15; under I, from I16 through I30; under N, from N31 through N45; under G, from G46 through G60; an under O, from O61 through O75.

- Bingo callers, situated in a central location, randomly select numbers from a drum that contains and "tumbles" all seventy-five numbers—for example, B9.
- Bingo players then check their cards, marking a box if the number called appears there.
- The caller will continue to "tumble" and select numbers until the winning sound blast of "Bingo!" is heard, and the card is verified.

- Once the winner has been established, a prize is awarded.
- If there is more than one winner, the prize is divided evenly among the winners.
- Depending on the rules as stated at the beginning of each game, winning bingo could be one line running vertically, horizontally, diagonally or a pattern.
- Coverall, or blackout, is a winning bingo that covers all the numbers on that particular card.
- Pattern bingo is a specified pattern on the bingo card. For example, the letters X, T, or H.

Bingo Strategies

For each game, other than progressives, there will always be a winner; therefore, bingo is one of the better gambling bets.

- Be sure to establish bingo as soon as the winning number is called.
- Listen and react quickly to the called number because if you miss any number you reduce or eliminate your chances of winning.
- Do not play more cards than you can comfortably manage.
- Your odds of winning are calculated by dividing the total number of cards released for that game by the number of cards you are playing. So if 1,000 cards are released and you have purchased 10, your chances of a win are 1 in 100.
- When selecting your cards and favorite numbers, here are some numbers that seem to come up more often: B1 – B10, I19 – I29, N31 – N39, G49 – G55, and O61 – O68.

Bingo Etiquette: The Dos and Don'ts of the Game

- Do relish every win with a loud and clear BINGO!
- Do choose some favorite numbers.
- Do participate in this happy social event.
- Don't brag about your winnings.
- Don't whine about your losses.
- Don't take a fellow player's lucky seat.

• Don't blame the caller. He or she is just the messenger.
• Do put Bingo on your "to do" list.

Bingo Facts

• Bingo is the most popular game in the world and a reliable fundraiser.
• There are 1,474,200 bingo card possibilities.
• Research has proven that bingo keeps you in peak mental form; physical exercise will tone up the body, but bingo players' mental speed, observation skills, and memory are enhanced by the game.
• Bingo keeps your mind and memory alert while providing an enjoyable social event.
• A game similar to bingo was utilized as a teaching tool in German schools to help children learn their multiplication tables.

Bingo Lingo

Caller: A person who calls out bingo numbers as they tumble from the holder.

Coverall: A winning bingo that covers all the numbers on a particular card. Also called blackout.

Dauber: A foam-tipped marker filled with ink for recording numbers called; available in fun colors and shapes. Daubers are the only acceptable method of marking paper cards in bingo halls.

Electronic dauber: Electronic dauber systems are now used extensively in bingo halls to play multiple packs of bingo cards at once.

Free space: The center square of the bingo card. This freebie is counted even if required for a pattern or coverall win.

Game board: A display board that reflects the bingo balls in play. It can also show the type of game currently being played and the size of the available jackpots.

Game variations: Double bingo, triple bingo, coverall, progressives, and hardway. Each has specific rules and is listed in your game program.

Hall ball: The first number drawn at the beginning of the bingo session. If this number is the winning number in any later game, a progressive jackpot is won along with the usual award for that particular game.

Hardway bingo: A one-line game won without utilizing the free space. Double hardway bingo requires two lines filled without utilizing the free space.

Jackpot: The prize awarded for a particular game or pattern win. A progressive jackpot grows until it is won and requires a separate buy-in. These games start with forty-five numbers drawn per session and go up one number per week until there's a winner. These are generally the first game played per bingo session.

Minimum buy-in: The least dollar amount paid in order for a player to be eligible for prizes.

Money ball: A number drawn before the game that doubles your winnings if bingo is called on that number.

Pattern bingo: A game in which the object is to fill a specified pattern on the bingo card. For example, the letters X, T, or H.

Rainbow pack: An assorted package of paper bingo cards that are played for various prize amounts. Blue cards are the least expensive, then red, then green, with tan paying the top bucks.

Squares: Patterns for bingo wins. The outside square utilizes the B and O columns plus the top and bottom rows. The inside square is a win around the free space utilizing columns I, N, and G.

Validation: After a called bingo, the player's card is checked to determine his or her eligibility for the jackpot award.

Wild number: These can be played for a double bingo, and are determined by the first number out. For example, if the first number is G47, all numbers ending in 7 will qualify as a wild number and should be marked.

WOB: Wild on Bingo. An expression created by the writer to end this glossary.

Bingo Trivia

- Bing Crosby was known as Bingo as a child.
- Screeno, a form of bingo, was played in movie theaters during the Depression.
- The casino game of keno is based on bingo.

- Most bingo gamers also like to play slot machines.
- The majority of bingo players have a pet, most often a cat.

Bingo Whimsy

Superstitions abound in the game of bingo. I list some of them below.

- Many players have a lucky bingo seat.
- Many players have lucky numbers.
- Many players have a lucky day and time for a bingo session.
- Many players have lucky charms, shoes, shirts, or ties.
- Lucky charms include rabbits' feet, elephants, teddy bears, frogs, monkeys, and gemstones.
- Pictures of loved ones, particularly grandchildren, are often on display at that lucky seat.
- Many players purchase daubers in their lucky color and/or in the shape of their lucky charms.
- Long-time players don't leave money on the table. It's bad luck.
- Many players walk in a circle around their chairs three times to ward off bad luck.

Bingo Online

This is the easiest and most comfortable way to play this fun game. You will find a display board for bingo numbers, along with the game pattern for a particular game. In most cases, the numbers are marked for you and a bingo immediately recognized. This is cyberspace fun accompanied by great graphics. Bingo is now played enthusiastically online around the world.

Bingo the British Way

The Brits offer a unique form of bingo, and the invented lingo is a real treat for the ears—veddy, veddy amusing. While the game has been around for a long time, the 1960s brought the birth of members' clubs, providing bingo sessions with plenty of pounds as prize money. The game is played with ninety bingo balls. A player must get five numbers in a row, column, or diagonal for bingo. You are then required to yell "House" or "Here" to stop the game.

Okay, mates, here's a sampling of British bingo lingo; these are the slang phrases for the numbers 1 through 90.

1   Kelly's Eye or At the Beginning
2   Me and You or Little Boy Blue
3   Cup of Tea, Dearie Me, or I'm Free
4   Knock at the Door or On the Floor
5   Man Alive or Jack's Alive
6   Tom's Tricks or Chopsticks
7   Lucky or God's in Heaven
8   Garden Gate or One Fat Lady
9   Doctor's Orders
10 Tony's Den or Uncle Ben
11 Legs Eleven
12 One Dozen or Monkey's Cousin
13 Unlucky for Some or Devil's Cousin
14 Valentine's Day
15 Young and Keen or Rugby Team
16 Sweet 16 or Never Been Kissed
17 Dancing Queen or Old Ireland
18 Coming of Age or Key of the Door
19 Good-bye Teens
20 One Score or Getting Plenty
21 Key of the Door or Royal Salute
22 Two Little Ducks or Dinky Doo
23 Thee and Me or A Duck and a Flea
24 Two Dozen
25 Duck and Dive
26 Pick and Mix or Half a Crown
27 Gateway to Heaven
28 Overweight or In a State
29 Rise and Shine or You're Doing Fine
30 Dirty Gerty or Blind Thirty

31	Get Up and Run
32	Buckle My Shoe
33	Dirty Knee or All the Threes
34	Ask for More
35	Jump and Jive
36	Three Dozen
37	More Than Eleven or A Flea in Heaven
38	Christmas Cake
39	Steps or All the Steps
40	Naughty Forty or Two Score
41	Time for Fun or Life's Begun
42	Winnie the Pooh or Famous Street in New York
43	Down on Your Knees
44	Droopy Drawers or All the Fours
45	Halfway There or Halfway House
46	Up to Tricks
47	Four and Seven
48	Four Dozen
49	P.C. or Copper
50	Half a Century or Bull's-Eye
51	Tweak of the Thumb or I Love My Mum
52	Danny LaRue or Weeks in a Year
53	Stuck in the Tree
54	Clean the Floor
55	Snakes Alive or All the Fives
56	Was She Worth It?
57	Heinz Varieties
58	Make Them Wait or Choo Choo Thomas
59	Brighton Line
60	Five Dozen or Three Score
61	Baker's Bun
62	Turn on the Screw or Tickety Boo
63	Tickle Me
64	Red Raw or The Beatles' Number
65	Old-Age Pension
66	Clickety-Click or All the Sixes

67 Made in Heaven
68 Saving Grace
69 Either Way Up or Meal for Two
70 Three Score and Ten
71 Bang on the Drum
72 Six Dozen
73 Queen Bee
74 Candy Store
75 Strive and Strive
76 Trombones
77 Sunset Strip
78 Heaven's Gate
79 One More Time
80 Eight and Blank
81 Stop and Run
82 Straight on Through
83 Time for Tea
84 Seven Dozen
85 Staying Alive
86 Between the Sticks
87 Torquay in Devon
88 Two Fat Ladies
89 Nearly There
90 Top of the Shop

As a gaming writer, I recommend this low-cost form of gambling as a good bet. Enjoy bingo, and may your winning number be the "last call."

To conclude my picks for the ten best bets, I'll introduce you to another game that has an immense popularity outside of casinos, and has been brought into them for that reason: sports betting.

Sports Betting
Holds the Line at Ten

14

My last best bet is not traditionally a casino game, but many casinos now have sports books (large areas that televise and "book" sports bets), because so many casino-goers like to wager on their favorite sporting events, such as football, basketball, baseball, hockey, and boxing. A sports book is not limited to these events, however. Any debatable event or topic, anything that can be bet on—such as who will win a presidential election—can have a "betting line."

Three sports betting definitions follow, with some lingo thrown in:

The betting line or money line (sometimes first appearing as a "morning line") is established by the casino itself or purchased from a company or individual (an "oddsmaker") who calculates, or "makes," betting lines.

The casino's commission, or vigorish, is built into the winning bets, just as it is with a banker's bet at the baccarat table.

The player bets not against the casino but against other players. The casino simply collects the vigorish in return for establishing the line and booking the bets. The main goal of the sports book is to maintain the betting line in a place where the money will be wagered as evenly as possible on both sides. Thus the casino does not pay out more money than it takes in; its profit comes wholly from the vigorish.

Therefore, it is the linemaker's job in creating the betting line to utilize a method of handicapping that will penalize the favorite bet and strengthen the opposition bet. This betting line can rise or fall right up to the start of the contest, allowing the casino sports book to gather as many bets as possible on the underbet team, thereby, eliminating "steam" (heavy action on one side) and establishing a profit no matter who wins the contest.

You lay, or give odds when betting the favorite, thus laying (or giving) a large bet to win a small amount; you take odds on the underdog ("dog"), making small wager to win big.

For example, let's imagine that the line has been set at 8–5 for a baseball game between the Arizona Diamondbacks and the Toronto Blue Jays during the World Series in the year 2020. (This is not so far-fetched after the results of the 2006 World Series, so indulge me with this example.) If I wager or lay odds on the favored Blue Jays (they have won this title twice, back in the 1990s, while Arizona has done so only once; thus the edge) with a wager of $8, the win will pay me $13 ($8 + $5).

However, taking odds and betting on the Diamondbacks will cost me $5 and return $12 for the win. I know you are asking, why not $13? Because the casino wants its commission—the "juice," or vigorish.

You can now see how the casino lures you in with the promise of winning more dollars when betting on the underdog, but there are many success stories derived from wagering this way, even with the additional risk involved. Sports book betting, like craps wagering, is one of the few bets where one can profit handsomely from a losing streak.

Point spread bet: Betting information for football, basketball, and hockey is quoted with the point spread (sometimes just called the "spread") on the big board.

The spread gives the underdog extra points, thereby challenging the favorite bettor to bet not just on the win, but to win by more than the point spread. This is called "covering" the spread, or "beating" the spread. A bet on the underdog wins if the underdog wins or if the favorite wins by less than the spread.

If the favorite meets the spread exactly, the game is a tie (push) for the point spread bet, and all wagers are returned. (For this reason, the line is often set in ½ point increments.)

You are always laying odds on a point spread bet for whatever side you choose, thereby paying more (for example, $11 to win $10). The house gets its vig (5 percent).

I'd say that's a lot, yes? But the house does provide a lot in return.

For instance, when you bet you lock in a particular price, regardless of any future changes in the line. This method, in most cases, protects your bet and is a wise decision to avoid receiving lower payouts in the future. You can buy ½ points (plus or minus; usually three is the limit) by accepting the odds that go along with them. (For example, to change a spread from +3 to +3 ½ or from -7 to -6 ½ on a bet of $100, you must risk $120 to win $100, instead of $110.)

A total bet: a wager on the total number of points scored by both teams during the game, based on an over or under quoted number. The big sports board explains these three bets, and quotes betting information as follows:

- The spread bet is listed first, with the home team in capital letters and the favorite team listed first. The actual point spread number will either be quoted in the minus (-10) for the favorite or plus (+10) for the underdog.

- Line bets are calculated for those bettors who want to bet on the final outcome of the contest only and are quoted for the favorite-laying odds or the underdog-taking odds. The casino's percentage (PC) is equal on spread and line bets.

- Total bets are laid based on the quoted total number of points scored. OV = betting over what the board offers; UN = under-betting that the teams won't score that many points together.

Strategies and Wager Management

I used to think that only mathematical or computer geniuses got ahead in this game. But while you definitely have to do your homework, spend some time on research, and analyze sports statistics, I found after hanging around Nevada sports book lounges (they are comfy, and great places to watch sporting events, aren't they?) that even novices can become handicappers extraordinaire by practicing sound wager management and discipline, as with any other casino game. I owe many thanks to the veteran handicappers at four Laughlin casinos for their input and expertise for this book.

Sports Book Glossary

Bookie: Bookmaker, or a person who takes bets.
Chalk: The favorite bet.
Circled game: A game where the betting limits are lowered, generally because of injuries and/or weather.
Cover: You win by more points than you laid or lose by more points than you took with a point spread win.
Dog: The underdog in the game.
Even money: A bet where one side lays no juice or vigorish.
Futures: Bets made today that take place at a later date.
Getting down: Placing your bet.
Hedge: To decrease the action by betting the opposite of a previous bet.
Juice: The commission that goes to the house; also known as vigorish.
Lines: Game odds.
Parlay: A bet with two or more teams in which all teams must win or cover for the bettor to win and receive higher payouts.
Pick: An even game, as there is not a favorite.
Point spread: The number of points the favorite gives the dog for betting purposes.
Push: A point spread tie.
Rundown: Listing of odds on a specific game day.
Straight bet: One wager, not a parlay (bet with two or more teams).
Sucker bet: Refers to methods used by bookies to lure rookies to bet more.
Teaser: A bet where you can adjust the point spread your way.
Total: A bet on the number of points scored in a game; one can bet over or under.

Sports Book Strategy

The biggest mistake sport bettors make is following their heart rather than their head, betting on hometown or favorite teams, or on sentimental favorites (a fighter or a horse one is attached to) when the odds are stacked against them.

Quality bets require research, starting with the newspaper sports section, sports magazines, the Internet, and the many TV sports channels (not tough so far—this is something you probably do every day). The best bets require substantial up-to-the-minute information as well. When you bet on sports, you are betting that your information is more accurate than other sports bettors'. In order to win, you have to be right!

So before betting you need to develop and to ask detailed questions, beginning with the following: Is there a team playing that you are more knowledgeable about? If so, focus on that team's stats and your past knowledge to determine betting probabilities. Who is on the injured list, and how will that affect the outcome of the game? Who has the home-field advantage, and how much does this mean to each team? Which teams win more away games? Who's matched up again who, and who's more likely to succeed in that matchup? Who's the pitcher, and what is his ERA? How does he do against the opposing team? What are both teams' stats for the last ten games? What are the weather conditions? Are the star players and the rookies healthy and working to their potential?

Generally, linemakers are highly accurate when setting odds; however, your in-depth analysis could produce a real quality bet. Set up your own rating system for teams and bet only those games where you have observed a consistent trend. For example, when you believe that you have a better-than-average knowledge of a particular team, that gives you an edge over your rival sports bettors.

Betting early, before the lines are firmly established, and betting against the emotional (not rational) hometown fans are two excellent tips.

Sound wager management translates into setting limits and dividing your betting money for the season into weekly betting dollars.

Online and in Nevada, comparison shopping is a must, as a range of point spreads and quality bets can be found up and down the strip. A "loss leader," or casino promotional giveaway bet, can be deceiving. For these, casinos usually establish a cap and allow only small wagers.

By all means, take advantage of such offers; but keep in mind that the other bets at that casino are not necessarily as good, and continue to shop until you are satisfied.

When a game is circled, usually because of an injured player, and the books don't have time to adjust the line, either the betting is reduced or the game is taken off the board and no action is taken.

Think carefully about betting more than two games that are played at the same time.

Ask: Are they all quality bets? Can I stand to lose on all bets and still stay within my budget?

You have to win at least 53 percent of your point-spread bets to keep ahead of the house vig. I suggest that novice sport bettors "get down," placing simply a line bet on which team will win—after doing your homework, of course.

This will let you wade in slowly, as opposed to jumping in cannon ball style. Upon graduation, you can move forward to parlays and teaser bets, where multiple correct selections will bring in bigger profits. Futures betting is also for the real pros, betting on a team to go the distance, using odds that are based on that team's projected finish order.

That's it then, my top ten picks for successful casino gambling. But I can't conclude this introduction to gambling without emphasizing the ten worst bets in the casino—bets that all players who consider themselves educated gamblers should avoid.

The Ten Worst Bets in the Casino

15

Here are the ten worst bets—stay away from these!
No matter how much you like the games listed below, I suggest you avoid them. They spell disaster for your pocketbook.

They are statistically the worst bets in the house, and I have the percentages to prove it.

It isn't difficult for the educated, intelligent player to locate a substitute casino game or better strategy in order to avoid these much-less-profitable bets.

Worst Bet No. 1: Keno

The casinos really want you to play keno. Just look at how much floor space they devote to the game—almost as much as slots. Why is it, do you think, that you can't eat a meal in the casino without a keno runner nearby?

Could this be because the casino advantage starts at 25 percent, the highest house advantage of any casino game?

Check this out: Your chances of hitting eight for eight are 230,000 to 1, and hitting ten for ten is nine times harder than winning the lottery.

Casinos now offer a "ways" bet, or video keno, as a means to draw in uneducated gamblers. These optional bets don't increase your odds; nor do they change the fact that the house edge is still over 25 percent. In the long run, this truly is a no-win game.

Worst Bet No. 2: The Big Wheel

The house edge here is 15 percent.

This "game" (which is really just a big moneymaker for the casino) is usually found at the casino exits and entrances.

With the Big Wheel, looking at pictures of $5, $10, and $20 bills, you put your money down and hope to match the spin of the wheel.

Of course, the casino is hoping that as you leave, you throw down your last $20. That way they have succeeded in taking all your money.

Come on, folks. You know there are much better bets in the house. Besides, I hope you are never down to your last $20 on any gambling trip.

Worst Bet No. 3: Roulette's Five-Number Line Bet

Placing your chip on the intersection of the lines between 0 and 1 to cover 0, 00, 1, 2, and 3 pays 6–1. While the double-zero roulette wheel is bad enough, at a casino advantage of 5.26 percent, this particular bet tops the list of the worst roulette bets, with a house edge of 7.89 percent.

Worst Bet No. 4: Caribbean Stud Poker

The worst option in this game is the progressive meter, where an additional $1 wager leaves you hoping for a natural royal flush.

With 650,000-to-1 odds of hitting it, this game is just way too expensive. Another disadvantage is the fact that the game cannot be played without the dealer holding at least a king and an ace. Move over to mini-baccarat, pai gow poker, or three-card poker.

Worst Bet No. 5: Let It Ride

This popular game has a lot of fans, but the casino advantage sits at 3.5 percent, just over the acceptable 3 percent or less. With other choice card games to select, leave this one behind.

Worst Bet No. 6: Red Dog

Another game with a 3.5 percent casino advantage.

Now I know casino gamblers are going to play this card game and No. 4 and No. 5 no matter what I say. All I ask, however, is that you try the better table games and/or machines. Let's call it a social experiment performed for profits.

Worst Bet No. 7: Blackjack Without Basic Strategy

Don't give the house an advantage of more than 5 percent.

Worst Bet No. 8: Any Proposition Bet on a Craps Table

This includes field bets, hardways, and Big 6 and 8. The house advantage for these starts at 9 percent and rises to 16 percent. Don't get so caught up in the roar of the game that you lose track of the best bets.

Worst Bet No. 9: Video Poker with No Strategy and No Pay-Schedule Knowledge

Random play increases the casino's advantage way above 3 percent. So does playing a partial-pay instead of a full-pay machine, or less than the maximum number of coins. See the chapter on video poker.

Worst Bet No. 10: Straight Slots That Have Less Than a 98 Percent Payback

Take the time to search and test slots before giving up your money. For tips on how to do this, read the slots chapter.

You'll notice that some of the games mentioned (craps, slots, video poker, blackjack, and roulette) are on my recommended list of the ten best bets in a casino.

The difference is in how you play them.

Intelligent gamblers will know how to play these games to get the most value for their money.

A Comprehensive Guide to Comps

16

Let's talk comps—that's short for the complimentary things, or freebies, that you earn from casinos. Comps are a reward system for visiting a casino.

The following is an article I wrote in which I tried to approach the topic of comps in a fun and easy manner. I wore out my thesaurus while looking for words with comp in them. As you will see, I added a few new words to the English language.

Comps or complimentaries, for rooms, food, beverages, and other goodies are a casino's compensation to the loyal player. However, the player has to earn them, and learn the rules of the comp game. Just as you prepare before entering any casino, so too is a complete education part of your casino compbat training.

Slot club cards are your entrance pass to comp heaven, and table game players are included, too, as more casinos are patching you into the same rating system. Slot club cards now encompass all the games in the casino, and they're free!

Slots clubs were started in Atlantic City, where casino execs were very aware that quarter slot players could easily move next door to competing casinos. Some incentive to remain loyal to their casino was established.

This plastic marketing tool now comprises policy for most casinos worldwide. Read the casinos' literature, and determine which casinos give the most compromising bang for your buck.

You want to develop a best, better, and good complete listing of casinos. There is no complaint list, as it is only to your benefit as a player to join.

Compiling active status and total points, plus the redeemable value of your card, is mandatory for any competent player.

Analyze casino card offers for how they will compensate you in terms of the games you play, the surroundings, the dining offerings, "entertainment, and, particularly, cash back. What are you competing for? Free room, free food, free shows, playing coupons, promotional items such as take-home souvenirs, or cash back?

To compare, the rebates available are:

- All casinos have complied in the beverage category.
- RFB—room, food, and beverage, the king of comps—is all that any high roller, or "whale" could comprehend. However, with some limitations, low to medium players are eligible. The compcept is to reward all loyal slot players.
- Cash rebates—generally 6 cents to $1 for every $100 played. This should most certainly determine a casino's "rating" for your compliance list. Turn the tables and rate the casinos when comparing slot cards.
- Meal Comps—averaging one meal comp for every four hours of quarter machine play. I often ask for a meal comp after a jackpot win and have never been refused—the casino wants to keep you at the company store. Plus, there's no standing in line—you head straight for the VIP or "invited guest" short queue; looking composed as you pass other waiting diners.
- Room COMPs: Watch your mailbox for casino newsletters, companion room offers, or ways members can reserve rooms at the casino rate—generally a 50 percent reduction.
- Another component is entertainment goodies. Two-for-one week day show coupons and members' rewards can be a headliner show compin the mail.
- Promotional gifts such as dice, cards, caps, and T-shirts—and that's just for signing on. Your birthday greetings arrive with compatible meal, room, and cash coupons.

- Funbooks and "lucky bucks": compensation for table games. Put your bet down with these coupons and you've just reduced the house advantage. Ask for these when reserving your room, when registering, when your travel agent books your trip, or all three times. Swing by the front desk to pick up casino brochures or local freebie magazines in the larger casino areas and comp-clip.
- VIP compatible for active members—special handling just for you.

More complimentary tips:

- Ask, ask, and ask again—be nice—if you are comptitled.
- Make friends with the slot host. Ladies are more competent with the male slot hosts . . . get my drift?
- Call the toll-free number of your favorite casinos for updated comp-formation.
- Contact casino marketing or the events manager. Ask about your total points accumulated, the redeemable value, and upcoming special promotions, especially double or triple points days—an incomparable advantage of an active member's dreams.
- Two compers can reach their freebie goal faster; request two slot cards with the same name and membership compartment number and doublecomp those points.
- Participate in a companion run, hitting at least five casinos, joining as you go, and collect all the compoffers.
- It's a common miscompception among gamblers that you must lose money to qualify. Casinos want your time in their establishment—use those cards.
- Tracking your points involves all monies you put through machines, whether you are dropping coins or playing off your credits—it all computes.
- Look up, at the neon signs in the casinos' windows; that's where they advertise their best games and best payouts—all compliments of the house.
- Attaching a card to you is a good idea. I'm the one with the colorful twisted cord attached to me; I have lost my composure and nearly a vital body part at times when forgetting to remove my card.

- Finally, wager management should also be part of your complete education. Don't play just for comps, but do remember, comparatively, that a reduction in the cost of play increases your gambling bankroll.
- Compulsive gambling is bad, but compulsion is good for every casino player; not only will you have good luck but you are making your luck with competence.

Listing of Merged US Casino Cards

The current and probably lasting trend is to combine several casino properties under one named slot club card to form a megaclub.

As a member, you may use your card at all participating casinos to gather points. I have provided a listing below of nine megaclubs and their participating casino locations.

Harrah's—Total Rewards

Harrah's	Atlantic City, NJ
Showboat Casino	Atlantic City, NJ
Harrah's	Cherokee, NC
Harrah's	East Chicago, IN
Harrah's	Joliet, IL
Harrah's	Metropolis, IL
Bluffs Run	Council Bluffs, IA
Harveys	Council Bluffs, IA
Harrah's	Prairie Band and Mayetta, KS
Harrah's	St. Louis, MO
Harrah's	North Kansas City, MO
Harrah's	Lake Charles, LA
Harrah's	Shreveport, LA
Harrah's	New Orleans, LA
Harrah's	Tunica, MS
Harrah's	Vicksburg, MS

Harrah's Ak-Chin	Maricopa, AZ
Harrah's	Lake Tahoe, NV
Harrah's	Las Vegas, NV
Harrah's	Laughlin, NV
Harrah's	Reno, NV
Harveys Casino	Lake Tahoe, NV
Rio Casino	Las Vegas, NV
Harrah's Rincon	Valley Center, CA

Park Place—Connection Card

Atlantic City Hilton	Atlantic City, NJ
Bally's	Atlantic City, NJ
Caesars	Atlantic City, NJ
Claridge	Atlantic City, NJ
Caesars	Elizabeth, IN
Bally's	New Orleans, LA
Bally's	Tunica, MS
Grand Casino	Tunica, MS
Grand Casino	Biloxi, MS
Grand Casino	Gulfport, MS
Sheraton	Tunica, MS
Bally's	Las Vegas, NV
Caesars Palace	Las Vegas, NV
Caesars	Lake Tahoe, NV
Flamingo	Las Vegas, NV
Flamingo	Laughlin, NV
Las Vegas Hilton	Las Vegas, NV
Paris	Las Vegas, NV
Reno Hilton	Reno, NV

Isle of Capri—Isle One

Isle of Capri	Bettendorf, IA
Rhythm City	Davenport, IA
Isle of Capri	Marquette, IA

Isle of Capri	Boonville, MO
Isle of Capri	Kansas City, MO
Isle of Capri	Bossier City, LA
Isle of Capri	Lake Charles, LA
Isle of Capri	Biloxi, MS
Isle of Capri	Lula, MS
Isle of Capri	Natchez, MS
Isle of Capri	Tunica, MS
Isle of Capri	Vicksburg, MS
Isle of Capri	Black Hawk, CO

Mandalay Resorts—One Club

Grand Victoria	Elgin, IL
MotorCity	Detroit, MI
Gold Strike	Tunica, MS
Circus Circus	Las Vegas, NV
Circus Circus	Reno, NV
Colorado Belle	Laughlin, NV
Edgewater	Laughlin, NV
Excalibur	Las Vegas, NV
Gold Strike	Jean, NV
Luxor	Las Vegas, NV
Mandalay Bay	Las Vegas, NV
Monte Carlo	Las Vegas, NV
Nevada Landing	Jean, NV
Slots-A-Fun	Las Vegas, NV

MGM Mirage Card

MGM Grand	Detroit, MI
Beau Rivage	Biloxi, MS
Bellagio	Las Vegas, NV
Buffalo Bill's	Primm, NV
Golden Nugget	Las Vegas, NV
Golden Nugget	Laughlin, NV

MGM Grand	Las Vegas, NV
Mirage	Las Vegas, NV
New York, New York	Las Vegas, NV
Primm Valley Resort	Primm, NV
Treasure Island	Las Vegas, NV
Whiskey Pete's	Primm, NV

Station Casinos—Boarding Pass

Boulder Station	Las Vegas, NV
Green Valley Ranch	Henderson, NV
Palace Station	Las Vegas, NV
Red Rock	Las Vegas, NV
Santa Fe Station	Las Vegas, NV
Sunset Station	Henderson, NV
Texas Station	North Las Vegas, NV

Fiesta—Amigo Club

| Fiesta | Henderson, NV |
| Fiesta | Las Vegas, NV |

Ultimate Rewards Club

| Arizona Charlie's East and West | Las Vegas, NV |
| Stratosphere | Las Vegas, NV |

Coast Clubs in Vegas

Barbary Coast
Gold Coast
Orleans
South Coast
Suncoast

The Benefits of Comps

This article of mine is from the "Editor's Rant" section of Casino Players Ezine published twice a month online.

I do not understand why all slot players don't sign up for a club card at every casino they visit. What are they afraid of: Getting on a mailing list and receiving junk mail? Too much hassle? Or is it just "I value my privacy"?

Let us take these objections one at a time.

Here's the worst thing that can happen to you—you get "junk mail" offering free rooms or low rates, free food, cash vouchers, birthday greetings, plus promotional news. I will take that junk anytime!

Mailing lists are gold to casinos, so they are reluctant to share that information with other casinos that are not in their corporate group.

I know that slot hosts take their favorite clients' information when they move to another casino job, but so what—more freebies for you.

Gosh, you have to schlep over to the promotions booth to sign up and most of the time you'll get a free gift, cash or food voucher, or a casino promotion specifically for new members right then and there. Is that any more hassle that going to your bank or lifting up your mattress when you are gathering your gambling bankroll for a casino visit?

In fact, you are adding to that precious bankroll by participating "in the club." Cash back, free food, and free rooms are all monies that you can add to your gambling pot. By the way, when you sign up, get two cards with the same name, so you and your partner can play on the same card to increase those points.

My friends, as far as privacy—we lost that years ago.

You cannot hide within this wired and wireless world. (That's www to you.) You do not have to divulge your Social Security number, and yes, casinos are "tracking" your play, but that's to determine your qualifications for the many benefits of the card, not to "spy on you." I received an e-mail recently from a reader who frequents casinos and has never signed up for a slots card and wanted to know how. My reply: Make a beeline for the promotions booth in any casino and sign up now.

Let us all take a moment of silence for the points and freebies this reader and others have not received. Yikes, I cannot do it—it hurts my thrifty heart too much. Ouch!

Do not play just for comps, but do take advantage of the casino cards and the casinos, in this case. I do whenever I can. Comps can also be found at most Web sites for land-based casinos; or you can type in your favorite casino's name plus "comps" to locate more. The reliable slot club card is a surefire way to gather comp points, and many land-based casinos will sign you up online before your arrival.

Also, leave an e-message for a slot host with details to customize your trip beforehand.

Internet Gambling

17

In this chapter, we will explore Internet gambling with a "to look for" list in locating reputable online casinos, payment options, promotions and bonuses, and suggested sites that will further assist in your selection. The principals of gambling discussed throughout this book should help you with online gambling itself, and online sites, especially free sites, can be excellent ways of test-driving your table skills.

There are two major types of sites—sports books and casinos—although most sites combine the two to create a total gaming package.

An initial deposit is requested, and many online casinos offer free play or discounts for new players. Sports books generally require higher deposits and minimum bets.

For security, most large sites are randomly audited by the larger reputable accounting firms, resulting in an ongoing project. Accounting firms are allowed round-the-clock access to these particular sites—definitely a good thing.

Here are a few things to look for when selecting an online casino:

- Contact: Toll-free phone number, e-mail, and fax. The more the better, and plan to do a test to see how they respond.
- Are the online casino phone operators knowledgeable, polite, and eager to assist you?
- Is your e-mail replied to in a timely fashion, with a personal

response, not a crappy form letter?

- Size of the operation: Do they have enough phone lines and customer service reps to get your questions or concerns answered in a timely fashion? A tip-off is if the same people always answer your call. That may indicate undercapitalization within the operation. Do they speak your language?
- Many online casino gambling establishments offer a "play for free" option. Some online casinos offer a better interface and more games than others do.
- Convenience and fast payout of your funds is of paramount importance. If you wish to withdraw funds from your account, how fast do they transfer your money? If they are surly or give you a hard time, asking you why you want your money, immediately withdraw all your cash and close your casino gambling account, then find another casino.
- How easy is it to view your account? Is the account accurate or are there "clerical" errors? Always keep track of your account cash balance so you can monitor the results.
- Check the speed with which funds and bets are posted and the accuracy of your wagers made.

Online Casino Deposit Options

Because some Visa/Mastercard/Paypal accounts are not accepted online, some slot machine players encounter difficulties depositing money into their casino accounts; however, there are many new online payment methods. Below are secure and safe payment companies that most casinos accept:

- NETeller is the leader; it is fast and easy. Opening a NETeller account is like using an online wallet. You can deposit, withdraw, and transfer funds to any participating merchants utilizing Visa, MasterCard, electronic funds transfers, bank deposits or wire transactions. NETeller provides same-day payments and virtually instant cash transfers. Best of all you pay no charges for transfers.

- PrePaid ATM is a service available to players in the United States only. When you apply for a PrePaid ATM card, you receive both a real card and a virtual card. The card acts as an ATM card, debit card, and money transfer card all in one.
- FirePay is an excellent choice and is very easy to sign up for; it takes only five minutes with step-by-step instructions. It's a free service that works like an ATM debit card.
- Wire transfer is the electronic transfer of money from your bank account into the relevant casino's electronic merchant bank account.
- Other options: Securebuxx, GPX Card, 900 Line Pay, Citadel Commerce, bank drafts, deposits via FedEx, Western Union, and online checks.

www.ecogra.org: A Watchdog Organization

The independent standards authority of the online gaming industry is eCOGRA, a non-profit organization specifically overseeing fair gaming, player protection, and responsible operator conduct. The function that eCOGRA performs protects those who engage in online gaming where it is lawful. A directory of approved sites can be found at their site.

I recommend that you look for the eCOGRA membership seal before playing at an online casino. With governments worldwide trying to put the brakes on Internet gambling, it's best that you make sure Internet gaming is legal where you live before you lay your money down.

I know it's a jungle out there, with a multitude of online casinos. To untangle this spider's web, I set some rules and went off on a quest for gambling directories to locate the best bets online.

I looked kindly on sites that not only offered top casino recommendations and bonuses but also answered any security or payment questions and loaded their pages with lots of "gambling stuff."

So, where does a newbie online slot player go in search of the best offerings? My suggestions follow:

- www.jackpotcentral.com is packed with information. Some of their directory choices include: Payout Percentages for Top 10, 2004 Best Casino, Casino Reviews, and an audited Casino Ranking Chart that includes current promotions and slot payouts.

- www.takevegashome.com: Click on New Players, where you will find resources to assist with your first online gaming experience.

- www.allgam.com lives up to its name with "everything you always wanted to know about gambling." A small sampling of their extensive directory includes the topics: Best Casinos or Sportsbooks, Fantasy Games, Lotteries, Play for Fun, Stock Market Betting, Travel, Free Casino Games, Free Casino Money, Glossary, and Not Recommended List.

- www.slot-machine.net brings you the ABC's of slot machine games online and a directory that reads in part: Top Online Slots, Top Slot Bonuses, Top Slot Payouts, and Top Online Jackpots. Mix in a slot education with selections of: Slot Categories, Free Slot Games, Slot History-Tips-Myths, and Book Reviews. There is also a Beginners Guide to answer those pressing questions: how to play slots, your first gamble, manage your money, and privacy issues, plus a handy checklist. Be sure to click on the article "Slot Machine Playing Tips: 13 Common-Sense Tips That Will Keep You from Becoming a Casino Victim Every Time You Try Your Luck at the Slots."

- www.webcasinocomps.com is a must-see for the mountain of in formation provided. It states that "all casinos listed offer free casino games, best odds, free casino cash bonuses and excellent customer service and they outline the criteria to be listed." Each casino must be fully licensed in the base country; offer twenty-four hour customer support; payouts must be certified; monetary transactions must be encrypted and paid in a timely manner. Top casinos for the current month are listed in detail; plus, the Web casinos are divided based on the initial bonus offered to new players.

- www.jackpotmonitor.com gives space to all the online software companies and their products. Find: Boss Media, Cryptologic, Diamond Digital, iCrystal, IQ-Ludorum, Microgaming, Net Entertainment, Playtech, Proprietary, Real Time Gaming, and World Gaming. In addition, the best and current online bonuses, slots and jackpot recommendations are posted.

Disclaimer: I am not an affiliated member of or associated in any way with these Web sites—just impressed with their online gaming presentations.

Three kinds of online casino bonuses are:

1. No-Deposit Bonus
    No-deposit bonuses offer a great way to test a casino's games without any risk. Most offer around $10 to try their games. Simply download and install the software or try the no-download games, claim the bonus, and give them a go. Most of the time you are restricted to withdrawing the winnings only. The bonus is meant to encourage you try the games and not a way people can claim some free cash by going after the bonuses.

2. First-Deposit Bonus
    Many online casinos offer bonuses when your make your first deposit. These range from 25 percent to 100 percent of the first deposit and may carry, depending on the deposit method used. Currently the more attractive bonuses are being offered for Western Union and wire-transfer deposits. Always read the fine print carefully, as there are usually minimum wagering requirements. This means that you must wager a certain amount—for example, four times the amount of your deposit plus bonuses—before you can withdraw the bonus. Others offer a more attractive bonus but it can't be withdrawn. Just read the conditions and make sure you track each bet to know how much you have wagered.

3. Ongoing Bonus
    Unlike land casinos, online casinos are not as easily able to offer free

meals and other benefits. There aren't a lot of online casinos that offer meaningful comp programs. Some will allow you to accumulate points that can be redeemed online, while others just give you some free cash.

- www.tradesports.com: Here is the site that gets the trophy for most unusual and downright interesting. TradeSports is a trading and betting exchange registered in Ireland and is a person-to-person exchange, not a sports book. You play against passionate sports fans who offer far better odds than a sports book. Make an offer. You can offer odds to others on any line you see or wager against any team or player who you think will lose. The usual sports of baseball, football, soccer, rugby, horse racing, and even cricket are on the board, but after that is where it gets interesting. You can take your chances on almost anything: the stock market, current events, international events, the world of entertainment, and, of course, the winner of the next American Idol competition. Play the stock market or "trade and chat" in the TradeSports forum. There's lots of fun, with new trades listed frequently. How about? When is the next Megabucks fortune going to hit?

When comparing online and land-based casinos, you'll notice that the "grounded" casinos offer more amenities and dining choices, plus a larger inventory of games with comping opportunities. Online gaming, however, provides a varied game selection, bonuses and promotions, easy access, and the comfort of playing in your pajamas. The choice is yours to discover, with an online hookup and the suggestions above.

Good luck, and may the "click be with you."

Casino Security

18

A casino vacation for fun, relaxation, and the "profitable" possibilities can be ruined if you're not being watchful of your own security. Most people are safety- and security-conscious at home; therefore, vacation time should be no different.

The short list for casino players that follows will help to ensure that you have a "safety shield" when casino hopping—particularly women who are gambling alone.

- Women: Do not bring your purses to the casino. Wear a waist purse or fanny pack when gambling; not only are your credit cards, personal identification, and money safe, but your hands are free for games and machines.
- When gambling alone, ask a security guard to escort you to your car when you leave, or use valet parking in the larger gambling areas. Two bucks for valet parking is a cheap price to pay for safety, considering that most casino parking lots are not well lit or well patrolled. When staying overnight, insist on a room close to the elevator and use the hotel safe for valuables.
- Don't take large payouts in cash; ask for a cashier's check to be issued by the casino. Resist the temptation to brag about your huge win or count your bills at the cashier's cage, in an elevator, or on the casino floor.
- Be wary of people who suddenly become your friend after a big win,

and check that you are not being followed around the casino or outside. Also, beware of pickpockets.

- Airports that serve nearby casinos require additional safety measures. Don't get distracted by strangers with unusual questions. The scam is set up by one person, who gets your attention with inane questions or chatter, while the other grabs and disappears. Be sure that your expensive luggage, laptop computer, or camera is within your view or watched by someone at all times.
- Check to see if there is a pass-through to the other side's bank of machines from where you are playing. Scam artists can reach through from the opposite side to the shelf beside your machine and grab the coin bucket you placed there.
- I have noticed that more casinos, especially in Nevada and Atlantic City, now have partitions to stop this crime. However, if there are not partitions, it's best to hold your bucket of coins on your lap as a precaution.
- Watch for the "drop the coins in front of you" scam, where you are distracted, offer to help, and find that your bucket of money is being removed. Today, TITO (Ticket In, Ticket Out) technology requires players to hang on tight to these tickets. Do not forget to pick up that ticket upon cashing out. The best strategy is to cash out quickly.
- Craps table rails make for easy snatches, as the players are very involved and distracted in this fast-paced game. Hold your money in your hands, or pocket it for safety.

Although the casinos try to be helpful and don't like the nightmares that customers' stolen money can bring, those surveillance cameras are watching the casinos' money, not yours!

The "Do's" of Casino Gambling

19

This is usually where a list of don'ts pops up, too. But, you know, I wouldn't want readers to get a negative feeling about intelligent gambling. Besides, we're all practical adults here. And I think gambling don'ts have been done to death. You know what they are.

So let's allow common sense to be your guide and explore the dos of gambling instead.

DO play games and make bets that have a casino advantage of less than 3 percent. Investigate new games for casino advantage percentages.

DO set aside a bankroll for each gambling session and play only that amount during that session.

DO practice progressive betting, pressing your bet after any win.

DO practice frequent cash-outs of your credits on slot and video poker machines.

DO ask questions. Most dealers and change staff are friendly and helpful. They want you to win, too. After all, your win often contributes to their tip.

DO continue your gambling education. Knowledge is the key, and you can never learn too much. Plus, in the gambling industry, the tide changes constantly. Continuing education will help you stay up to date on new games, new rules, and new strategies.

DO get excited about small wins and break-even wins. Enjoy what you're doing. Remember: Luck is preparation meeting opportunity.

DO shop for value. Look for the best games, dealers, machines, and casinos and for games with simple features.

DO move around. Try this machine, that table game over there. Diversity keeps the boredom away. Exercise your body and brain at the same time.

DO take up the casino challenge in a fair fight. May the winning prize be yours!

Casino Pet Peeves

20

As much as I enjoy spending time at my favorite casino and hotels, and I have visited my share, it seems that often, the annoyance factor also accompanies me.

Here is my list of pet peeves. Aren't you annoyed by writers who use lists?

This list is in no particular annoyance-factor order; I dislike all of them without bias.

- Those eternal lines at the cashier cages. With TITO (ticket in, ticket out), coins have almost disappeared in most casinos today; the eternal lines, alas, have not. I want my coins in crisp bills—fast! Of course, I always get in the slowest line. You have a nice win to cash out, but you are not so lucky when selecting which line to stand in. Many casinos have adopted the one-line, first-available-cashier approach—good idea.
- Those blasted coin buckets that don't fit under the spewing coin tray without tossing coins all over the floor.
- Casinos set up in such a maze of crisscrossing aisles that you have to be a rocket scientist to find the exits. During this search, you are regaled by the constant "Wheeeeeel of Fortune" chant in the casino. Can we kill or at least soften that sound? And while we are talking about the setup of the casino floor, would it be too much to ask for more restrooms?

- Faulty machines that are not replaced—the buttons stick or come off in your hand as you try desperately to hold a card. Some screens are so blurred or "sunburnt" that you can barely see what is going on in front of you.
- Casino employees who continue to serve drinks to someone who really does not need "one for the road." It's just good PR and good guest relations to put these clients in cabs and thank them for visiting.
- Casino or hotel check-ins that take more than ten minutes.
- Casino security: All single women should automatically get a room next to the elevator without asking and receive an immediate response when requesting an escort to their car. Parking lots that are not well lit and well patrolled are another irritation. At least there's an easy answer for this one: Use valet parking at all times—the few bucks are worth the peace of mind. Just remember there's no need to loudly announce your room number or how much money you are counting out.
- Blackjack rules: Not only do the rules change from casino to casino, but since when should six to eight decks, burning ten to fifteen cards, and mid-game shuffling be attractive to me as a player? When I show the least inclination toward playing intelligently, casino management reserves the right to remove me from the property.
- A "hot" craps table that suddenly comes to a grinding halt because dealers decide that it is time to "ask questions." Does this game have a rhythm to it? You bet. Does this ploy affect the shooter? Often. Do the dealers know this? Bet your last buck on it!
- MegaJackpots that are paid out over twenty years, or paid up front at a huge discount to the "winner."
- "Certified" or guaranteed slots not clearly marked. And why are there not loads of these slots everywhere?
- Keno runners—give me some credit for knowing that this is the worst bet in the house. Or do I have to wear a sign declaring, "I don't play Keno" to be left alone?
- Machine hogs: Read the message: "One machine per customer at busy times." Don't these people know that when slots are placed side by side, rarely do they both pay? And when you finally do get to play

your favorite machine, you are treated to the "foaming at the mouth" onlooker who will hover until you surrender.

- Casino players who touch the screen after enjoying their latest snack, bang on it, caress it, or—the worst—talk to their newest acquaintance: the slot machine. People who leave little mementos after exiting the slot, like cigarette butts or ashes, wrappers, any old garbage—not an appreciated gift.
- Unfriendly or uninformed staff. "I don't know" or "we don't offer that" should not be part of the vocabulary for any hotel or casino representative. A decent, living wage so that staff members are not constantly groveling for tips should be high on casino management's "to do" list.
- Casino or hotel management who are not in touch with customers' wants, needs, and dislikes concerning all aspects of their gaming establishment. Take a poll, offer comment cards with a free gift for completion, use your club-card mailings for feedback, place a suggestion box in a visible area, teach your staff the art of customer satisfaction, and ask them to approach customers for their opinions.

What can we, as casino players, do about the annoyance factor? Plenty—start by being vocal, in a nice way, and make sure that top management people hear your advice.

Write a quick note about your complaints and leave it in your room or at the front desk.

An avalanche of patrons' complaints cannot be ignored for long.

I believe all is not lost, that casino management can and will change. We just need to nudge them in the right direction before they completely forget what the words "customer service" means. All of us have the right to enjoy every casino experience.

The Final Roundup

21

Here we are at the end of the tour, and I sincerely hope that your casino gambling knowledge has been enhanced by what you've read.

Readers and fans asked me to make this an easy read. I met this challenge by teaching only the best strategies and games—keep it simple, ma'am! I do hope your motto now is: Become able, and profit will follow . . . a winner!

Of course, I know that this doesn't end your casino gambling education, nor mine. I can still walk into any casino or browse online and learn something new, and I'm sure it will always be that way.

In a more philosophical mode, I offer the following advice:

Remember, the two hardest times to leave a casino are when you're ahead and when you're behind.

Know thyself and play within yourself whenever you arrive in a casino, for only you can explain what creates a positive gaming experience for you, and as you come to understand your reasons better and get educated, you will evolve into a happy winner.

Casinos should and do make money. What galls me is that they prey upon uneducated players by changing the rules of the games or by bringing in inferior takeoffs or new versions of games and machines that invariably up the casino percentage above the 3 percent that intelligent gamblers strive to stay under.

That's the battle right there. Keep up the good fight—you intelligent players!

May Lady Luck smile on you.

She usually gives me a big grin and a wink.

U.S. Casino Recommendations

22

As a gambling writer, I have been fortunate to visit many of the casinos in the United States, and I'm happy to share my recommendations with you.

There are more than 1,600 gaming locations in the States, including casinos, racinos, horse and dog tracks, and cruise ships. As the gambling industry booms across America, a casino gambler's choices need not be restricted to Nevada any longer. The three largest gambling venues outside of Nevada are Atlantic City, Mississippi, and the largest casinos in the world—Foxwoods and nearby Mohegan Sun.

Although the New Orleans area and Mississippi were hit hard by Hurricane Katrina in 2005, most of the casinos have returned and are now welcoming players.

These recommendations consider all casinos games but are primarily based on slots and video poker payout reporting.

These Las Vegas "Bests" are listed in no particular order. Play where the locals win.

Fiesta Rancho (northwest Vegas)
Rampart (formerly Regent—northwest Vegas)
Palms (off the Strip at Flamingo)
Fiesta Henderson
El Cortez (downtown)

Boulder Station (Boulder Highway)
Sam's Town (Boulder Highway)
Union Plaza (downtown)
Main Street Station (downtown)
Gold Coast (across from Palms)
Texas Station
Sunset Station

Listed in order of top casino picks by casino name or region:

Reno: Peppermill, Atlantis, and Harrah's
Laughlin: Harrah's, Golden Nugget, and River Palms
Atlantic City: Borgata, Harrah's, Trump Marina
Colorado: Best Regions, Cripple Creek, Central City, and Blackhawk
Connecticut: Foxwoods and Mohegan Sun (These two very competitive casinos vie for the best payouts, and the vote usually comes out a tie.)
Illinois: Casino Queen, Grand Victoria, and Alton Belle
Indiana: Argosy, Belterra, and Caesars.
Iowa: Prairie Meadows, Dubuque, and Diamond Jo
Louisiana: Best regions: Shreveport or Bossier, Baton Rouge, and Lake Charles.
Missouri: President, Isle of Capri—Boonville and St. Jo Frontier
Mississippi: Best regions: Coastal, North, and South. (Mississippi is divided into regions. South = Vicksburg, Natchez, and Greenville. Coastal = Biloxi, Gulfport, and Bay St. Louis. North = Tunica, Robinsonville, and Lula.)
Detroit, Michigan: MGM Grand, Greektown, and MotorCity.

There is a toll-free listing with Web sites for all the major US casinos on the pages that follow.

U.S. Casinos: Nevada, Mississippi, Atlantic City, and California

Toll-free numbers, Web sites and locations for Nevada, Mississippi, Atlantic City, and California casinos. All information is correct at the time of this writing but may change.

164

Nevada

Las Vegas	Toll-Free Number	Web Site
Aladdin	877-333-9474	www.aladdincasino.com
Arizona Charlie's East	888-236-9066	www.azcharlies.com
Arizona Charlie's West	800-342-2695	www.azcharlies.com
Ballys	800-7-BALLYS	www.ballyslv.com
Barbary Coast	888-227-2279	www.barbarycoastcasino.com
Bellagio	888-987-6667	www.bellagioresort.com
Boulder Station	800-981-5577	www.stationcasinos.com
Caesars Palace	800-634-6661	www.caesars.com
California	800-634-6505	www.thecal.com
Cannery	866-999-4899	www.cannerycasinos.com
Circus Circus	800-634-3450	www.circuscircus.com
El Cortez	800-634-6703	www.elcortezhotelcasino.com
Excalibur	800-937-7777	www.excaliburcasino.com
Fiesta Henderson	866-469-7666	www.stationcasinos.com
Fiesta Rancho	800-731-7333	www.stationcasinos.com
Fitzgeralds	800-274-5825	www.fitzgeralds.com
Flamingo Las Vegas	800-732-2111	www.flamingolasvegas.com
Four Queens	800-634-6045	www.fourqueens.com
Gold Coast	888-402-6278	www.goldcoastcasino.com
Gold Spike	800-634-6703	www.goldspikehotelcasino.com
Golden Gate	800-426-1906	www.goldengate.com
Golden Nugget	800-634-3403	www.goldennugget.com
Hard Rock	800-HRDROCK	www.hardrockhotel.com
Harrah's	800-392-9002	www.harrahs.com
Hyatt, Lake LV	800-55HYATT	www.lakelasvegas.hyatt.com
Lady Luck	800-LADYLUCK	www.ladylucklv.com
Las Vegas Club	800-634-6532	www.playatlv.com

Imperial Palace	800-634-6441	www.imperialpalace.com
Las Vegas Hilton	800-732-7117	www.lvhilton.com
Luxor	800-288-1000	www.luxor.com
Main Street Station	800-465-0711	www.mainstreetstation.com
Mandalay Bay	877-632-7000	www.mandalaybay.com
MGM Grand	800-929-1111	www.mgmgrand.com
Mirage	800-627-6667	www.themirage.com
Monte Carlo	800-311-8999	www.montecarlo.com
MonteLago	877-553-3555	www.casinomontelago.com
New York-New York	800-693-6763	www.nynyhotelcasino.com
Orleans	800-ORLEANS	www.orleanscasino.com
Palace Station	800-544-2411	www.palacestation.com
Palms	866-942-7777	www.thepalmslv.com
Paris	888-BONJOUR	www.paris-lv.com
Plaza	800-634-6575	www.plazahotelcasino.com
Railroad Pass	800-654-0877	www.railroadpass.com
Rampart	866-999-4899	www.rampartcasino.com
Red Rock	866-767-7773	www.redrocklasvegas.com
Rio	800-PLAYRIO	www.playrio.com
Riviera	800-634-6753	www.rivierahotel.com
Sahara	800-634-6666	www.saharahotelandcasino.com
Sam's Town	800-634-6371	www.samstown.com
San Remo	800-522-7366	www.sanremolasvegas.com
Santa Fe	866-767-7770	www.stationcasinos.com
Silverton	800-588-7711	www.silvertoncasino.com
South Coast	866-796-7111	www.southcoastcasino.com
Stratosphere	800-99TOWER	www.stratospherehotel.com
Suncoast	866-636-7111	www.suncoastcasino.com
Sunset Station	888-319-4655	www.sunsetstation.com

Terribles	800-640-9777	www.terribleherbst.com
Texas Station	800-654-8888	www.texasstation.com
Treasure Island	800-944-7444	www.treasureislandlasvegas.com
Tropicana	888-826-8767	www.tropicanalv.com
Tuscany	877-887-2261	www.tuscanylasvegas.com
Venetian	888-283-6423	www.venetian.com
Westin Casuarina	800-228-3000	www.starwood.com
Wynn	888-320-WYNN	www.wynnlasvegas.com

Laughlin	Toll-Free Number	Web Site
Colorado Belle	800-477-4837	www.coloradobelle.com
Edgewater	800-677-4837	www.edgewater-casino.com
Flamingo	888-662-5825	www.flamingolaughlin.com
Golden Nugget	800-237-1739	www.gnlaughlin.com
Harrah's	800-HARRAHS	www.harrahs.com
Pioneer	800-634-3469	www.pioneerlaughlin.com
Ramada Express	800-243-6846	www.ramadaexpress.com
River Palms	800-835-7903	www.rvrpalm.com
Riverside	800-227-3849	www.riversideresort.com

Reno	Toll-Free Number	Web Site
Atlantis	800-723-6500	www.atlantiscasino.com
Bordertown	800-443-4383	www.bordertowncasnorv.com
Cal Neva	877-777-7303	www.clubcalneva.com

Circus Circus	800-648-5010	www.circusreno.com
Eldorado	800-648-5966	www.eldoradoreno.com
Fitzgeralds	800-535-LUCK	www.fitzgeraldsreno.com
Harrah's	800-HARRAHS	www.harrahsreno.com
Peppermill	800-648-6992	www.peppermillcasinos.com
Reno Hilton	800-648-5080	www.renohilton.com
Sands Regency	800-648-3553	www.sandsregency.com
Silver Legacy	800-687-7733	www.silverlegacy.com

Lake Tahoe	Toll-Free Number	Web Site
Caesars	800-648-3353	www.caesars.com
Harrah's	800-HARRAHS	www.harrahs.com
Harveys	800-553-1022	www.harrahs.com
Horizon	800-322-7723	www.horizoncasino.com
Hyatt Regency	800-553-3288	www.laketahoehyatt.com
Lakeside Inn	800-523-1291	www.lakesideinn.com
Tahoe Biltmore	800-BILTMOR	www.tahoebiltmore.com

Mississippi

North: Tunica and Lula	Toll-Free Number	Web Site
Bally's	800-382-2559	www.ballyms.com
Fitzgeralds	800-766-LUCK	www.fitzgeraldstunica.com
Gold Strike	888-24KPLAY	www.goldstrikemississippi.com
Grand Tunica	800-946-4946	www.grandtunica.com
Harrah's	800-HARRAHS	www.harrahs.com

Hollywood	800-871-0711	www.hollywoodtunica.com
Horseshoe	800-303-7463	www.horseshoe.com
Isle of Capri	800-789-5825	www.isleofcapricasino.com
Sam's Town	800-456-0711	www.samstowntunica.com

Vicksburg, Natchez, and Greenville	Toll-Free Number	Web site
Harrah's	800-843-2343	www.harrahs.com
Isle of Capri, Natchez	800-THEISLE	www.isleofcapricasino.com
Isle of Capri, Vicksburg	800-THEISLE	www.isleofcapricasino.com
Rainbow	800-503-3777	www.rainbowcasino.com

Coastal: Biloxi, Gulfport, and Bay St. Louis	Toll-Free Number	Web Site
Beau Rivage	888-750-7111	www.beaurivageresort.com
Boomtown	800-627-0777	www.boomtownbiloxi.com
Casino Magic, Biloxi	800-5MAGIC5	www.casinomagic.com
Casino Magic, St. Louis	800-5MAGIC5	www.casinomagic.com
Copa Casino	800-946-6272	www.thecopacasino.com
Grand Biloxi	800-946-2946	www.grandbiloxi.com

Imperial Palace	800-436-3000	www.ipbiloxi.com
Isle of Capri, Biloxi	800-843-4753	www.isleofcapricasino.com
Palace	800-PALACE9	www.palacecasinoresort.com
President	800-THEPRES	www.broadwater.com
Treasure Bay	800-PIRATE9	www.treasurebay.com

Atlantic City

Casino	Toll-Free Number	Web Site
Atlantic City Hilton	800-257-8677	www.hiltonac.com
Bally's and Wild Wild West	800-225-5977	www.ballysac.com
Borgata	866-692-6742	www.theborgata.com
Caesars	800-443-0104	www.caesarsac.com
Harrah's	800-2HARRAH	www.harrahs.com
Resorts	800-336-6378	www.resortsac.com
Showboat	800-621-0200	www.harrahs.com
Tropicana	800-THE-TROP	www.tropicana.com
Trump Marina	800-365-8786	www.trumpmarina.com
Trump Plaza	800-677-7378	www.trumpplaza.com
Trump Taj Mahal	800-825-8888	www.trumptaj.com

California

Casino	Toll-Free Number	Web Site
Agua Caliente	866-858-3600	www.hotwatercasino.com
Augustine	888-752-9294	www.augustinecasino.com
Barona	888-7BARONA	www.barona.com

Black Oak	877-747-8777	www.blackoakcasino.com
Cache Creek Casino and Resort	800-452-8181	www.cachecreek.com
Cher-Ae Heights Casino	800-684-BINGO	www.cheraeheights.com
Chuckchansi	866-794-6946	www.chuckchansigold.com
Chumash Casino	800-728-9997	www.chumashcasino.com
Colusa Casino	800-655-UWIN	www.colusacasino.com
Coyote Valley	800-332-9683	www.coyotevalley.com
Eagle Mountain	800-903-3353	www.eaglemtncasino.com
Elk Valley	888-574-2744	www.elkvalleycasino.com
Fantasy Springs	800-837-2-WIN	www.fantasyspringsresort.com
Feather Falls	877-OKBINGO	www.featherfallscasino.com
Gold Country Casino	800-334-9400	www.gold-country-casino.com
Golden Acorn	866-794-6244	www.goldenacorncasino.com
Harrah's Rincon	877-777-2457	www.harrahs.com
Havasu Landing	800-307-3610	www.havasulanding.com
Hopland Sho-Ka-Wah	888-746-5292	www.shokawah.com
Jackson Rancheria	800-822-WINN	www.jacksoncasino.com
Konocti Vista Casino	800-FUN-1950	www.kvcasino.com
Lucky Seven Casino	866-777-7170	www.lucky7casino.com
Morongo	800-252-4499	www.casinomorongo.com

171

Paiute Palace	888-3PAIUTE	www.paiutepalace.com
Palace Indian Gaming	800-942-6886	www.thepalace.net
Paradise	888-777-4946	www.paradise-casinos. com
Pechanga	888-PECHANGA	www.pechanga.com
Robinson Rancheria	800-809-3636	www.robinsonrancheria. biz
Rolling Hills	888-331-6400	www.rollinghillscasino. com
San Manuel	800-359-2464	www.sanmanuel.com
Soboba Casino	888-772-SOBOBA	www.soboba.net
Spa Casino	888-258-2-WIN	www.sparesortcasino. com
Sycuan	800-279-2826	www.sycuancasino.com
Table Mountain	800-541-3637	www.tmcasino.com
Thunder Valley	866-871-7771	www.thundervalleyres ort.com
Trump 29	800-841-6666	www.trump29.com
Twin Pines	800-564-4872	www.twinpine.com
Valley View	866-726-7277	www.valleyviewcasino. com
Viejas	800-84-POKER	www.viejas.com
Win River Casino	800-280-8946	www.win-river.com

U.S. Casinos: Other

Midwest Casinos—Seven States

Includes Illinois, Indiana, Iowa, Michigan, Minnesota, Missouri, and Wisconsin

Illinois Casinos	Toll-Free Number	Web Site
Alton Belle Riverboat	800-336-SLOT	www.argosycasinos.com

Casino Queen	800-877-0777	www.casinoqueen.com
Empress Argosy	888-4-EMPRESS	www.argosycasinos.com
Grand Victoria Casinos	847-888-1000	www.grandvictoria-elgin.com
Harrah's Joliet Casinos	800-HARRAHS	www.harrahs.com
Harrah's Metropolis	800-935-7700	www.harrahs.com
Hollywood Casino, Aurora	800-888-7777	www.hollywoodcasino-aurora.com
Jumers, Rock Island	800-477-7747	www.jumerscri.com
Par-A-Dice	800-DEAL-ME-IN	www.par-a-dice.com
Indiana Casinos	**Toll-Free Number**	**Web Site**
Argosy	888-ARGOSY7	www.argosycasinos.com
Belterra	888-BELTERRA	www.belterracasino.com
Blue Chip	888-879-7711	www.bluechip-casino.com
Caesars Indiana	888-766-2648	www.caesarsindiana.com
Casino Aztar, Evansville	800-DIAL-FUN	www.casinoaztar.com
Grand Victoria	800-GRAND-11	www.hyatt.com
Harrah's East Chicago	877-496-1777	www.harrahs.com
Horseshoe Casino, Hammond	866-711-7463	www.horseshoe.com
Majestic Star	888-2B-LUCKY	www.majesticstar.com
Trump	888-21-TRUMP	www.trumpindiana.com
Iowa Casinos	**Toll-Free Number**	**Web Site**
Ameristar	877-462-7827	www.ameristarcasinos.com
Argosy Casino, Sioux City	800-424-0080	www.argosycasinos.com
Bluffs Run	800-BET2WIN	www.harrahs.com

Catfish Bend	800-372-2WIN	www.catfishbendcasino.com
Diamond Jo	800-LUCKYJO	www.diamondjo.com
Dubuque Greyhound Park	800-373-3647	www.dgpc.com
Harrah's Council Bluffs	800-HARRAHS	www.harrahs.com
Isle of Capri, Bettendorf	800-747-5825	www.isleofcapricasino.com
Isle of Capri, Marquette	800-496-8238	www.isleofcapricasino.com
Lakeside	877-477-5253	www.lakesidecasino.com
Meskwaki	800-728-4263	www.meskwaki.com
Mississippi Belle 2	800-457-9975	www.belle2casino.com
Prairie Meadows	800-325-9005	www.prairiemeadows.com
Rhythm City	800-BOAT-711	www.rhythmcitycasino.com
Winnavegas	800-468-9466	www.winnavegas-casino.com
Michigan Casinos	**Toll-Free Number**	**Web Site**
Greektown	888-771-4386	www.greektowncasino.com
MGM Grand	877-888-2121	www.detroit.mgmgrand.com
MotorCity	877-777-0711	www.motorcitycasino.com
Bay Mills	800-4BAYMILLS	www.4baymills.com
Chip-In's	800-682-6040	www.chipincasino.com
Kewadin (five locations)	800-KEWADIN	www.kewadin.com
Kings Club	888-422-9645	www.baymills.com
Lac Vieux	800-583-3599	www.lacvieuxdesert.com

Leelanau Sands	800-922-2946	www.casino2win.com
Little River	888-568-2244	www.littlerivercasinos.com
Ojibwa	800-323-8045	www.ojibwacasino.com
Soaring Eagle	888-7EAGLE7	www.soaringeaglecasino.com
Turtle Creek	888-777-8946	www.casino2win.com
Victories	877-442-6464	www.victories-casino.com
Minnesota Casinos	**Toll-Free Number**	**Web Site**
Black Bear	888-771-0777	www.blackbearcasinohotel.com
Canterbury Park	800-340-3661	www.canterburypark.com
Fond-du-Luth	800-873-0280	www.fondduluthcasino.com
Fortune Bay	800-992-7529	www.fortunebay.com
Grand Casino, Hinkley	800-472-6321	www.grandcasinosmn.com
Grand Casino, Mille Lacs	800-626-5825	www.grandcasinosmn.com
Grand Portage Lodge	800-543-1384	www.grandportagemn.com
Jackpot Junction	800-WINCASH	www.jackpotjunction.com
Mystic Lake	800-626-7799	www.mysticlake.com
Northern Lights	800-252-7529	www.northernlightscasino.com
Palace	800-228-6676	www.palacecasinohotel.com
Prairies Edge	866-293-2121	www.prairiesedgecasino.com

Seven Clans Red Lake	888-679-2501	www.sevenclanscasino.com
Seven Clans Thief River Falls	800-881-0712	www.sevenclanscasino.com
Sevens Clans War Road	800-815-8293	www.sevenclanscasino.com
Shooting Star	800-453-STAR	www.starcasino.com
Treasure Island	800-222-7077	www.treasureisland.com
White Oak	800-653-2412	www.whiteoakcasino.com
Missouri Casinos	**Toll-Free Number**	**Web Site**
Ameristar Kansas City	800-449-4961	www.ameristarcasinos.com
Ameristar St. Charles	800-325-7777	www.ameristarcasinos.com
Argosy	800-900-3423	www.argosycasinos.com
Aztar	800-679-4945	www.casinoaztarmo.com
Harrah's, North Kansas City	800-HARRAHS	www.harrahs.com
Harrah's, St. Louis	800-HARRAHS	www.harrahs.com
Isle of Capri, Boonville	800-THEISLE	www.isleofcapricasino.com
Isle of Capri, Kansas City	800-946-8711	www.isleofcapricasino.com
Mark Twain	866-454-5825	www.casinomarktwain.com
President Casino	800-772-3647	www.presidentcasino.com
St. Jo Frontier Casino	800-888-2946	www.stjocasino.com
Wisconsin Casinos	**Toll-Free Number**	**Web Site**
Bad River	800-777-7449	www.badriver.com

Ho-Chunk	800-746-2486	www.ho-chunk.com
Lake of the Torches	800-25-TORCH	www.lakeofthetorches.com
LCO Casino or Convention	800-LCO-CASH	www.lcocasino.com
Majestic Pines	800-657-4621	www.mpcwin.com
Menominee	800-343-7778	www.menomineecasinoresort.com
Mohican North Star	800-952-0195	www.mohicannorthstar.com
Mole Lake Regency	800-236-WINN	www.molelake.com
Oneida	800-238-4263	www.oneidabingoandcasino.net
Potawatomi	800-PAYS-BIG	www.paysbig.com
Potawatomi, Northern Lights	800-487-9522	www.cartercasino.com
Rainbow	800-782-4560	www.rbcwin.com
St. Croix, Hole in the Wall	800-238-8946	www.stcroixcasino.com

More States

Arizona Casinos	Toll-Free Number	Web Site
Apache Gold	800-APACHE8	www.apachegoldcasinoresort.com
Blue Water	888-243-3366	www.bluewaterfun.com
Bucky's (two locations)	800-SLOTS44	www.buckyscasino.com
Casino Arizona Talking Stick–Salt River	877-724-HOUR	www.casinoaz.com
Casino of the Sun and Del Sol	800-344-9435	www.casinodelsol.com

Cliff Castle	800-381-SLOT	www.cliffcastle.com
CoCoPah	800-23-SLOTS	www.wincocopahcasino.com
Desert Diamond (two locations)	866-332-9467	www.desertdiamondcasino.net
Fort McDowell	800-THEFORT	www.fortmcdowellcasino.com
Gila River (three locations)	800-WINGILA	www.wingilariver.com
Harrah's Ak-Chin	800-HARRAHS	www.harrahs.com
Hon-Dah	800-929-8744	www.hon-dah.com
Mazatzal	800-777-7529	www.777play.com
Paradise	888-777-4946	www.paradise-casinos.com
Colorado Casinos	**Toll-Free Number**	**Web Site**
Bronco Billy's	877-989-2142	www.broncobillyscasino.com
Bullwhackers-Silverhawk	800-GAMBULL	www.bullwhackers.com
Double Eagle	800-711-7234	www.decasino.com
Famous Bonanza–Easy Street	866-339-5825	www.famousbonanza.com
Fitzgeralds	800-538-5825	www.fitzgeralds.com
Gold Rush–Gold Diggers	800-235-8239	www.grushcasino.com
Golden Gates	866-343-1994	www.goldengatescasino.com
Imperial Hotel	800-235-2922	www.imperialcasinohotel.com
Isle of Capri, Blackhawk	800-843-4753	www.isleofcapricasino.com
J.P. McGills	888-461-7529	www.triplecrowncasinos.com

Midnight Rose	800-635-5825	www.midnightrose.com
Sky Ute	888-842-4180	www.skyutecasino.com
The Lodge at Blackhawk	877-711-1177	www.thelodgecasino.com
Ute Mountain	800-258-8007	www.utemountaincasino.com
Womacks Legends	888-966-2257	www.womackscasino.com
Connecticut Casinos	**Toll-Free Number**	**Web Site**
Foxwoods	800-FOXWOODS	www.foxwoods.com
Mohegan Sun	888-226-7711	www.mohegansun.com
Delaware Casinos	**Toll-Free Number**	**Web Site**
Delaware Park	800-41SLOTS	www.delpark.com
Dover Downs	800-711-5882	www.doverdowns.com
Midway	888-88SLOTS	www.midwayslots.com
Florida and Georgia Cruises	**Toll-Free Number**	**Web Site**
Big M	888-373-3521	www.bigmcasino.com
Key West Cruises	866-874-PLAY	www.kwcasinocruises.com
La Cruise	800-752-1778	www.lacruise.com
Miccosukee	800-741-4600	www.miccosukee.com
Palm Beach Princess	800-841-7447	www.pbcasino.com
St. Tropez Cruises	800-575-5520	www.sttropezcasinocruises.com
Sea Escape	877-SEAESCAPE	www.seaescape.com
Seminole Brighton	866-2CASINO	www.seminoletribe.com
Seminole Hard Rock, Hollywood	800-937-0010	www.seminolehardrock.com
Seminole Hard Rock, Tampa	800-282-7016	www.seminoldhardrock.com
Seminole Hollywood	800-323-5452	www.seminoletribe.com

Sterling Casino Lines	800-ROLL711	www.sterlingcasinolines.com
Sun Cruz (Five locations)	800-474-DICE	www.suncruzcasino.com
Emerald Princess, Georgia	800-842-0115	www.emeraldprincesscasino.com
Millionaires Casino, Georgia	800-630-0390	www.millionairescasino.net
Louisiana Casinos	**Toll-Free Number**	**Web Site**
Bally's Lakeshore New Orleans	800-57-BALLY	www.ballysno.com
Belle of Baton Rouge	800-676-4847	www.argosycasinos.com
Boomtown Bossier	866-462-8696	www.boomtowncasinos.com
Boomtown Westbank	800-366-7711	www.boomtowncasino.com
Casino Rouge, Baton Rouge	800-44-ROUGE	www.casinorouge.com
Cypress Bayou Casino	800-284-4386	www.cypressbayout.com
Grand Casino Coushatta Kinder	800-584-7263	www.gccoushatta.com
Harrah's Casino New Orleans	800-HARRAHS	www.harrahs.com
Harrah's Lake Charles	800-977-PLAY	www.harrahs.com
Harrah's Louisiana Downs	800-HARRAHS	www.deltadowns.com
Harrah's Shreveport	800-HARRAHS	www.harrahs.com
Hollywood Shreveport	877-602-0711	www.hollywoodcasinoshreveport.com
Horseshoe, Bossier City	800-895-0711	www.horseshoe.com
Isle of Capri Casino, Bossier City	800-475-3847	www.isleofcapricasino.com

Isle of Capri Casino, Lake Charles	800-THE-ISLE	www.isleofcapricasino.com
Paragon	800-946-1946	www.paragoncasinoresort.com
Treasure Chest, New Orleans	800-298-0711	www.treasurechest.com
New Mexico Casinos	**Toll-Free Casino**	**Web site**
Big Rock Casino	866-244-7625	www.bigrockcasino.com
Camel Rock	800-GO-CAMEL	www.camelrockcasino.com
Cities of Gold	800-455-3313	www.citiesofgold.com
Dancing Eagle	877-440-9969	www.dancingeaglecasino.com
Isleta Gaming Palace	800-843-5156	www.isletacasinoresort.com
Ohkay	800-PLAY-AT-OK	www.ohkay.com
San Felipe Hollywood	877-529-2946	www.sanfelipecasino.com
Sandia	800-526-9366	www.sandiacasino.com
Sky City	888-SKY-CITY	www.skycitycasino.com
Taos Mountain	888-WIN-TAOS	www.taosmountaincasino.com
North Carolina, North Dakota, and New York Casinos	**Toll-Free Number**	**Web Site**
Harrah's Cherokee (NC)	800-HARRAHS	www.harrahs.com
Dakota Magic (ND)	800-325-6825	www.dakotamagic.com
Four Bears (ND)	800-294-5454	www.4bearscasino.com
Prairie Knights (ND)	800-425-8277	www.prairieknights.com
Sky Dancer (ND)	866-244-9467	www.skydancercasino.com

Spirit Lake (ND)	800-WINUBET	www.spiritlakecasino.com
Akwesasne (NY)	888-622-1155	www.mohawkcasino.com
Seneca Allegany (NY)	877-553-9500	www.senecaalleganycasino.com
Seneca Niagara (NY)	877-873-6322	www.snfgc.com
Turning Stone (NY)	800-771-7711	www.turningstone.com
Oklahoma Casinos	**Toll-Free Number**	**Web Site**
Cherokee Casino (Three locations)	800-760-6700	www.cherokeecasino.com
Choctaw Casino (Six locations)	800-788-2464	www.choctawcasinos.com
Comanche Nation (Three locations)	866-354-2500	www.comanchenationgames.com
Creek Nation (Four locations)	800-299-2738	www.creeknationcasino.com
Gold River Bingo Casino	866-499-3054	www.westerndelaware.nsn.us
Remington Park	800-456-9000	www.remingtonpark.com
The Stables	877-774-7884	www.the-stables.com
Thunderbird Wild Wild West	800-259-5825	www.okthunderbirdcasino.com
Oregon Casinos	**Toll-Free Number**	**Web Site**
Chinook Winds Casino	888-CHINOOK	www.chinookwindscasino.com
Kah-Nee-Ta High Desert	800-238-6946	www.kahneeta.com
Kla-Mo-Ya Casino	888-552-6692	www.klamoya.com
The Mill	800-953-4800	www.themillcasino.com

The Old Camp Casino	888-343-7568	www.oldcampcasino.com
Seven Feathers	800-548-8461	www.sevenfeathers.com
Spirit Mountain	800-760-7977	www.spiritmountain.com
Wild Horse	800-654-9453	www.wildhorseresort.com
South Dakota Casinos	**Toll-Free Number**	**Web site**
Cadillac Jack's	866-332-3966	www.cadillacjacksgaming.com
Deadwood Gulch	800-695-1876	www.deadwoodgulch.com
First Gold	800-274-1876	www.firstgold.com
Four Aces	800-834-4384	www.fouracesdeadwood.com
Gold Dust Gaming	800-456-0533	www.golddustgaming.com
Mineral Palace	800-84-PALACE	www.mineralpalace.com
Old Style Saloon #10	800-952-9398	www.saloon10.com
Royal River	800-833-8666	www.royalrivercasino.com
Silverado Gaming	800-584-7005	www.silveradocasino.com
Tin Lizzie	800-643-4490	www.tinlizzie.com
Washington Casinos	**Toll-Free Number**	**Web Site**
7 Cedars Casino	800-4LUCKY7	www.7cedarscasino.com
Chewelah	800-322-2788	www.chewelahcasino.com
ClearWater	800-375-6073	www.clearwatercasino.com
Emerald Queen Riverboat	888-831-7655	www.emeraldqueen.com
Little Creek	800-667-7711	www.little-creek.com

Lucky Eagle	800-720-1788	www.luckyeagle.com
Muckleshoot Casino	800-804-4944	www.muckleshootcasino.com
Northern Quest	888-603-7051	www.northernquest.net
Quinault Beach	888-461-2214	www.quinaultbchresort.com
Red Wind	866-946-2444	www.redwindcasino.net
Silver Reef	866-383-0777	www.silverreefcasino.com
Skagit Valley	877-275-2448	www.theskagit.com
Tulalip	888-272-1111	www.tulalipcasino.com
Two Rivers	877-7COME11	www.tworiverscasinoandresort.com
Yakima Nation	877-7COME11	www.yakimalegends.com
West Virginia Casinos	**Toll-Free Number**	**Web Site**
Charlestown Races	800-795-7001	www.ctownraces.com
Mountaineer	800-804-0468	www.mtrgaming.com
Wheeling Island	877-WINHERE	www.wheelingdowns.com

We're now on our way north of the border to visit Canadian casinos. Hang on.

Canadian Casinos

North of the Border for Fun and Games

23

Gambling in Canada expanded in leaps and bounds during the 1990s. Currently, there are 38,000 Video Lottery Terminals (VLT), more than 31,000 slot machines, more than 32,000 lottery ticket centers, and 107 horse-racing teletheaters.

Canada boasts 59 casinos and 70 racetrack or slots venues in seven provinces and the Northwest Territories. Provincial governments oversee gaming in each of the participating provinces.

The legal gambling age is nineteen. Call ahead for casino hours and location. All information below is correct at the time of this writing but may change.

Nova Scotia
VLTs allowed at licensed bars in the province.

Sheraton: 1969 Upper Water St., Halifax, NS, on the waterfront—Purdy's Wharf.

Quebec
All casinos have a dress code (no jeans); no gratuities are accepted.

Casino Montreal: 1 Ave. du Casino, Montreal, in Parc des Iles. Has a five-star restaurant.

Casino de Hull: 1 Blvd. du Casino, Hull. Across the river from Ottawa, Canada's capital city.

Ontario

Ontario Casino Corp: Call 416-326-0076 for current updates.
Charity Casinos: Four locations. All use the Winners Circle player's card.
Brantford: 40 Icomm Dr., Brantford. Located fifty-five miles southwest of Toronto in downtown Brantford, ON. This celestial-themed casino has a gift shop, a liquor license, the Meteor Bar lounge, and dining at the Cosmic Diner cafeteria. Open twenty-four hours.
Thunder Bay: 50 Cumberland St. South, Thunder Bay. Location: On the north shore of Lake Superior in Thunder Bay, ON. The area is rich in the history of mining, marine life, and fur trading. Has a seafaring-themed casino of fourteen thousand square feet.
Point Edward: 2000 Venetian Blvd., Point Edward. Location: Ten blocks from Sarnia, ON, near the Bluewater Bridge on the St. Clair River. Indoor sights of a ship's hull, a saltwater aquarium, and a glass bridge add to this nautical-themed casino.
Casino Sault Ste. Marie: 30 Bay St. West, Sault Ste. Marie. Location: Northern Ontario, approximately four hundred miles north of Toronto. Great hunting and fishing in this area. Eighteen racetracks are scheduled to install up to nine thousand slots as per the provincial plan in partnership with the Ontario Lottery and Gaming Corporation.

Manitoba
VLTs are available in many bars throughout Manitoba. Two of the best are:

Club Regent: 1425 Regent Street West, Winnipeg.
McPhillips Station: 484 McPhillips St., Winnipeg.

Saskatchewan

Casino Regina: Union Station, at 1880 Saskatchewan Dr., is this province's premier casino.

Alberta

Casinos offer regular slots rather than VLTs. Edmonton is Canada's fastest-growing gaming city, and Casino Yellowhead is its jewel. Edmonton is also the home of the world's largest shopping-and-entertainment complex, the West Edmonton Mall.

Casino Yellowhead: Yellow Head Trail at 153rd St. located in the West Edmonton Mall. At 73,500 square feet, Yellowhead is the largest casino in western Canada.

British Columbia

Great Canadian Casinos operates several casinos in British Columbia. Most locations offer these table games: blackjack, roulette, mini-baccarat, Red Dog, Let It Ride, Caribbean Stud Poker, Sic Bo, Texas Hold 'Em, Seven-Card Stud Poker, and slots. Each casino is centrally located in large municipalities and offers currency exchange, food and beverage service, wheelchair accessibility, and nearby public transportation.

Yukon Territory

Klondike Visitors Bureau: 867-993-5575.
Diamond Tooth Gerties: Dawson City; 867-993-5525. Open May through September.

The Western Canada Lottery Corporation works in conjunction with the provinces of Alberta, Saskatchewan, and Manitoba; the territory of Yukon, and the Sport North Lottery Authority.

There are no taxes paid on lottery or casino winnings in Canada.

Since I'm Canadian and was born in Toronto, the research for this information was a labour (Canadian spelling) of love.

Canada Casinos
(listed east to west by province)

Nova Scotia	Phone
Nova Scotia—Casino Halifax	888-6GAMES6
Casino Sydney	888-6GAMES6
Quebec	
Hull-Ottawa Casino	800-265-7822
Casino Montreal	800-665-2274
Casino Charlevoix	800-665-2274
Ontario	
Casino Niagara	888-946-3255
Casino Rama, Orillia	800-832-7529
Casino Windsor	800-991-7777
Blue Heron, Scugog	888-29HERON
Point Edwards Charity Casino, Sarnia	888-394-6244
Sault Ste. Marie Charity Casino	800-826-8946
Thunder Bay Charity Casino	877-656-4263
Brantford Charity Casino	519-752-5004
Manitoba	
Club Regent, Winnipeg	204-957-2700
McPhillips Station, Winnipeg	204-957-3900
Saskatchewan	
Union Station Casino, Regina	800-555-3189
Bear Claw, Gold Eagle, Northern Lights, and Painted Hand—First Nation Casinos	306-764-4777
Alberta	
Yellowhead Casino, Edmonton	780-424-WINS
Casino Edmonton	780-463-WINS
Palace Casino, Edmonton	780-444-2112

Casino Calgary	403-248-9467
Cash Casino, Calgary	403-287-1635
Casino Lethbridge	403-381-WINS
Jackpot Casino, Red Deer	403-342-5825
Gold Dust Casino, St. Albert	403-460-8092
British Columbia	
Great Canadian Gaming Corp. (8 locations)	604-303-1000
Casino Victoria	250-380-3998
Renaissance, Vancouver	604-682-8415
Holiday Inn, Vancouver	604-872-5543
Nanaimo Casino	250-753-3033
Richmond Casino	604-273-1895
Newton Casino, Surrey	604-543-8388
Casino View Royal, Vancouver Island	250-391-0311
Casino Coquitlam	604-523-6888
Lake City Casinos (Penticton, Kelowna, Kamloops, and Vernon)	250-861-5457

Ontario Racinos

Ontario racinos are open year-round and have machines in addition to horse and car racing. Overnight stays are not always available on-site but can be arranged for in nearby towns and cities. Nickel slots are not available.

Racino	Phone
Clinton Racetrack/Slots	519-482-7540
Dresden Racetrack/Slots	519-683-1551
Flamboro Downs, Dundas	905-628-4275
Fort Erie Racetrack/Slots	800-234-7987

Georgian Downs, Thornton	705-726-9400
Hanover Racetrack/Slots	519-364-7606
Hiawatha Slots, Sarnia	519-542-0134
Kawartha Downs, Fraserville	705-939-6316
Mohawk, Campbellville	800-732-2230
Rideau Carlton, Gloucester	613-726-3400
Sudbury Downs, Sudbury	705-855-7164
Western Fair Racetrack/Slots, London	519-672-5394
Windsor Raceway, Windsor	877-77-SLOTS
Woodbine Racetrack, Toronto	888-675-7223

International Casinos

The World's Finest

24

This section is for all the world travelers out there—and I count myself among you, as traveling is my second passion. New cultures, new vistas, new experiences—and now more countries have casinos. Double bonus! Let's explore.

This international casino travelogue highlights some of the finest and most elegant casinos in the world. After all, we do deserve the best, mais oui (but of course). Remember, when in Rome . . . observe the local customs and keep in mind that many international casinos are not open twenty-four hours.

Some casinos urge a proper to elegant dress code. If you stay away from shorts and jeans, you will get past the entranceway. Visiting a casino is considered a social event to a lot of people around the world, and one should dress accordingly.

Generally, international casinos cater to the tourist trade; therefore, in some areas, foreign tourists only are allowed, thereby bolstering the country's economy. There may be a small entrance fee.

Most foreign countries will ask for your passport for identification. That's their way of tracking undesirables, and is thus a benefit to you. The minimum age is usually twenty-one.

Call ahead, inquire at your travel agency, or search the Web as you plan your travels. The information is correct at the time of this writing but may change.

There are almost 3,000 gaming locations outside the United States and Canada, including casinos, racinos, horse and dog tracks, and cruise ships. The following pages divide the international casino properties into six regions: Caribbean, Europe, Asia, Central and South America, Oceania, and Africa.

At the beginning of each region, I list the total number of gaming locations in that area; list the countries in that area that have gaming locations; and order the list by number of gaming locations, with the highest first. For example, the Caribbean has 120 gaming locations, and the Netherland Antilles, listed first, has the most within the region.

Europe has 1,680 gaming locations, and France has the most, so it's listed first.

With such a large number of gaming locations, I utilized a selection process to narrow the list yet offer as wide a variety by country and continent as possible.

The process I used was based on these factors: a) four-star (or better) casino, b) size—the larger properties made the list, c) a Web site for more information, d)variety of games offered, and e) a preferred travel destination offering other sights to explore.

Following is a listing of the finest casinos worldwide by continent, country, and city, with addresses and telephone numbers.

Legend:

T=Telephone
HN=Not Open 24 Hours
HC=Hotel-Casino
SF=Size in Square Feet
D=Dress Code—Jacket Required
E=Entrance Fee Required
G=Games
B=Baccarat
BJ=Blackjack
C=Craps
P=Poker
R=Roulette

CSP=Caribbean Stud Poker
S=Slots (Includes VP)

Caribbean (120)

Netherlands Antilles, Dominican Republic, Puerto Rico, Antigua and Barbuda, Jamaica, Aruba, Bahamas, Martinique, Barbados, Trinidad and Tobago, Guadeloupe, Haiti, St. Kitts and Nevis, St. Vincent and the Grenadines, and Virgin Islands.

1. El San Juan Hotel and Casino, 6063 East Isla Verde Ave., Carolina, 00979, P.R. T=(787) 791-1000 or (800) 468-6659. HN, HC, SF=20,000.
www.thesanjuanhotel.com G=S, B, BJ, C, P, R, CSP.
Decorated with twenty-four-karat-gold-leaf ceiling, crystal chandeliers, mahogany-paneled walls, tuxedo-clad staff, elegant European style; unlike any other casino in the Caribbean. Spanish and English gaming instructions.

2. Atlantis Resort and Casino, Casino Drive, Nassau, Paradise Island, Bahamas. T=(242) 363-3000 and (800) 722-7466. HC, SF=100,000.
www.atlantis.com G=S, B, BJ, C, P, R, CSP.
Largest island resort in the world, a 14-acre waterscape; 100-foot underwater tunnel will allow viewing of all kinds of sea life overhead and around.

3. Renaissance Aruba Beach Resort and Crystal and Seaport, L. G. Smith Boulevard 82, Oranjestad, Aruba. T= +297 5-828731 and +297 5-836000. HC, SF=27,000. www.arubarenaissance.com G=S, B, BJ, C, P, R, CSP.
The casino also offers electronic bingo, and race book and sports book betting.

4. Holiday Beach Hotel and Casino Royale, Pater Euwensweg 31, Willemstad, Curacao, Netherlands Antilles. T=+599 9-462-5400. HN, HC, SF=29,900 www.hol-beach.com G=S, B, BJ, C, P, R, CSP.

5. Hotel Jack Tar Village, Playa Dorada, Puerto Plata, Dominican Republic. T=(809) 320-3800 and (800) 999-9182. HN, HC, SF=40,000. www.amcasgroup.com or puerto_plata.htm G=S, B, BJ, C, P, R, CSP. Languages: Spanish, English, German, and French.

Europe (1,680)

France, United Kingdom, Germany, Russia, Estonia, Czech Republic, Ireland, Netherlands, Latvia, Spain, Ukraine, Poland, Belarus, Finland, Switzerland, Croatia, Slovenia, Austria, Lithuania, Romania, Italy, Belgium, Greece, Bulgaria, Portugal, Serbia and Montenegro, Slovakia, Georgia, Macedonia, Denmark, Hungary, Sweden, Malta, Monaco, Moldova, Gibraltar, Norway, Albania, Andorra, Bosnia and Herzegovina, and Luxembourg.

With 1,680 casinos to choose from, I had to narrow the list to the top 15 casinos in Europe, considering the selection process as defined previously. All of the following are internationally renowned, as is the clientele. Jet-set, new and old money, rock stars, superstars. Celebrity spotting is not uncommon, especially for the common folk at these casino palaces. Vive la différence.

The ultimate European casino experience would have to be Monaco, the little principality tucked away on the French Riviera, and its capital, Monte Carlo. It's the playground for the rich and famous and the rest of us. Monaco is divided by the harbor facing the blue Mediterranean, the two areas being Monaco Ville, also known as the Rock, the old medieval city housing the Rainier palace, and our targeted destination of Monte Carlo.

While not open twenty-four hours, casinos do remain open until the wee hours of the morning.

1. Le Grand Casino de Monte-Carlo, Place du Casino, Monte Carlo, 98000 T=+377 92 16 2000. HN, D, E. www.monte-carloresort.com G=S, B, BJ, C, P, R. chemin de fer, punto banco Built in 1863 in "royal" style; period decorations. Bohemian glass chandeliers, rococo ceiling, lots of marble, gold fixtures, with tables of the finest wood and intricate design. Belle epoque architecture was popular during the reign of Napoleon III. Enter via the Atrium with its twenty-eight ionic

columns, and continue across the Renaissance Hall to the main gambling hall, divided into rooms, or salles.

Three other casinos nearby are: Monte Carlo Sporting Club and Casino, Monte Carlo Grand Hotel and Sun Casino, and Cafe de Paris, a grand hotel from yesteryear.

Monaco is a fairy tale come true for travelers, especially at night; and Monte Carlo, a must-see for gamblers. Although I was there many years ago, I can still close my eyes and remember the details. Maintenant, bonne chance, as we travel Europe.

2. Spain:
Casino de Mallorca, Ubanizacion Sol de Mallorca, Calvia, Mallorca, Illes Balears 07181 T= +34 971 130 000. HC, E, SF=172,200. www.casinodemallorca.com G=S, BJ, C, P, R. Formula 1 Club for high rollers.

Casino Gran Madrid, Torrelodones, Madrid de 28250. T=+34 900 900 810. HN, D, E, SF=110,000. www.casinogranmadrid.es G=S, BJ, R. Private gaming area, showroom and tournaments.

3. France:
Casino de Deauville, Rue Edmond Blanc, Deauville, Basse-Normandie 14800 T= +33 2 31 98 66 00. HN, HC, D, E, SF=44,000. www.lucienbarriere.com G=S, B, BJ, C, P, R. Punto banco.
Located approximately 90 minutes north of Paris on the Normandy beaches. Palatial is not a strong enough word; the outside view is reminiscent of the Palace de Versailles, set among carefully tended gardens. French and American roulette available. Le Regine's Disco extraordinaire. Racecourse, marina, regattas, and a sandy beach. The Promenade des Planches boardwalk extends along the seafront. Stay around for the evening spectacle when the lights go on and the diamonds come out to shine. Special events are scheduled for August 15 (Assumption) and, of course, July 14 (Bastille Day). Also, movie stars are easy to spot during the American Film Festival, held the first week in September. The population in the area can swell to 250,000. Nearby Trouville, a less tony sister city, also offers a casino.

4. Germany:
Spielbank Baden-Baden, Kaiserallee 1, Baden-Baden, Germany 76530
T=+49 722 302 40. HN, D, E, SF=32,000. www.casino-baden-baden.de
G=S, B, BJ, C, P, R.
Some gaming rooms are patterned after the imperial palaces of France. The
Winter Garden room is the inviting entrance to the casino: Austria Room,
Red Room, and Salon Pompadour are also impressive. The first casino in
Germany has seen many famous patrons: Aga Khan, Dostoyevsky, Kaiser
Wilhelm I. Marlene Dietrich said, "This is the most beautiful casino in
Europe." Gaming rooms open at different times. Blackjack 4–5 P.M., rou-
lette 2 P.M., American roulette 6 P.M., baccarat 3 P.M./6 P.M., poker 8 P.M.
Gaming lessons available. Casino tours are available. History, elegance, and
gaming tables all rolled into one tour. Famous hot springs nearby beck-
oned European royalty as far back as Roman times.

5. Italy:
Casino Municipale di Sanremo, Corso degli Inglesi 18, San Remo, Liguria
18038 Italy. T=+39 1845 340 01. HN, D, E. www.casinosanremo.it G=S,
B, BJ, R.
Location: Italian Riviera, 35 miles from Nice by Via Aurelia from Nice or
Genoa. Largest resort on the Italian Riviera. Turn-of-the-century European
style from when Alfred Nobel and Empress Maria Alexandrovna, wife of
Czar Alexander II, were patrons.

Casino de la Vallèe, Via Italo Mus, Valle d'Aosta, Saint Vincent, Valle d'Aosta
11027 Italy. T=+39 1665 221 or +39 1665 222 87. HN, HC, D, E,
SF=43,000. www.casinodelavallee.it G=S, BJ, P, CSP, R, chemin de fer, and
punto banco.
Northern Italy—55 miles North of Turin. Ultramodern high-roller heaven.
International celebrities are VIP card holders and gain entrance to the private salons. International ski resort and summer trout fishing.

6. Holland:
Holland Casino Scheveningen, Kurhausplein 1, Den Haag, Zuid-Holland
2587 RT Netherlands. T=+31 70 306 7777. HN, D, E, SF=97,000.

www.hollandcasino.nl G=S, B, BJ, P, CSP, R, punto banco.
Scheveningen is next to The Hague on the North Sea coast. Languages:
Dutch, French, English, and German. Slots, with large progressive jack-
pots, and bingo. Largest and most luxurious of the Dutch casinos.
Historic beach hotel, pier, and amusement park.

Holland Casino Amsterdam, Max Euweplein 62, Hirsch Passage 7, Amsterdam, Noord-Holland, Netherlands 1017 MB. T=+31 20 521 1111. HN, D,
E, SF=92,000. www.hollandcasino.nl G=S, B, BJ, P, CSP, R, punto banco
and sic bo. The largest casino in the city of Amsterdam.

7. Russia has more than 120 casinos. We highlight two of the premium
properites, one in Moscow and the other in St. Petersburg.

Carnival Casino, Zelioniy Prospect, 81, Moscow, Moskva 111558, Russian
Federation. T=+7 495 780 3457. SF=7500. www.superslots.ru\carnival
G=S, BJ, P, R.

Vegas Casino and Sports Bar, 6 Manezhnaya Square, St. Petersburg, 191011
Russian Federation. T=+7 812 710 5000. www.vegas.ru G=S, BJ, P, CSP, R,
Let It Ride, and pontoon.

8. Czech Republic:
Casino Bohemia, Prague Congress Centre, Palace of Culture, Tr. 5, Kvetna
65, Prague, Czech Republic. T=+420 241 412 587 or +420 261 174 116.
HN, D, SF=10,000. G=S, B, BJ, P, CSP, R.
The largest and most popular casino in the Czech Republic, located in
historic Prague.

9. Hungary:
Casino Las Vegas at Sofitel Budapest, 2 Roosevelt Terrace, Budapest 1051,
Hungary. T=+36 1 317 6022. D, E, SF=13,000. www.lasvegascasino.hu
G=S, BJ, P, R, punto banco.
Located in the historic castle district of Buda. The private gaming room is
in the tower of a 700-year-old monastery.

10. Finland:
Grand Casino Helsinki, Mikonkatu 19, Helsinki, Etela-Suomen 00100, Finland T=+358 9 680 800. HN, D, E, SF=29,000.
www.grandcasinohelsinki.fi G=S, BJ, P, R, punto banco and Red Dog.

11. Denmark: Casino Copenhagen, Amager Boulevard 70, c or o Radisson SAS Scandinavia Hotel Copenhagen, Denmark. T= +45 3396 596 5. HN, HC, D, E, SF=16,000. www.casinocopenhagen.dk G=S, BJ, P, R, punto banco. Located a half a mile from the Tivoli Gardens.

12. United Kingdom: Although, there are over 250 casinos located in Scotland, Wales, and England, no large Vegas-style casinos have arrived—yet. The Gala Group has many small locations offering slots and table games. Several cities are bidding for super casinos, including Cardiff, Coventry, Glasgow, Middlesbrough, Newcastle, Salford, and Sunderland. Further consideration goes to London's Wembley Stadium and Millennium Dome, Cardiff, Blackpool, Manchester, and Sheffield.

Asia (215)

Japan, Kazakhstan, Macau, Philippines, Cyprus, South Korea, Cambodia, Sri Lanka, Nepal, India, Israel, Armenia, Malaysia, Myanmar, Hong Kong, United Arab Emirates, Lebanon, Turkmenistan, Vietnam, Singapore, Kyrgyzstan, and Laos.

The countries of Macau, Nepal, and Philippines offer up the finest casinos in the Far East.

1. Macau:
Grand Emperor Hotel and Emperor Palace Casino, 288 Avenida Comercial de Macau Macau. T=+853 383 898. HC. www.grandemperor.com G=S, B, BJ, R. Casino Lisboa, 2-4 Avenida de Lisboa, Macau. T=+853 377 666. HC. www.hotelisboa.com G=S, B, BJ, R, boule, and fan-tan. Casino and Hotels in Macau cater to neighboring Hong Kong tourists. Macau is in transition now as big U.S. casino names vie for lucrative partnerships. Most of the smaller casinos will be closed as Vegas-style themes enter the market.

2. Nepal:
Hyatt Regency Kathmandu and Tara Casino, Taragaon Boudha Kathmandu, Nepal. T=+977 1 449 1234. HC, SF=21,000.
www.kathmandu.regency.hyatt.com G=S, B, BJ, CSP, pontoon.

Casino Anna, Durbar Marg, Kathmandu, Madhyamanchal, Nepal.
T=+977 1 228 650. HC, SF=12,000.
www.casinosnepal.com or casinonepal.html G=S, B, BJ, P, R, paplu.
There are a total of six casinos tucked away in this Himalayan splendor. All are at least four-star and are open 24 hours.

3. Philippines:
Hyatt Manila and Casino Filipino, Mabini cor, Pedro Gil Street, Malate Manila, National Capital Region 1004 Philippines. T=+63 (2) 245-9763. HC, SF=161,000. www.newpagcor.com or cf_hyatt.htm G=S, B, BJ, P, R.

Casino Filipino Pavillion, Holiday Inn Manila Pavillion Hotel, United Nations Avenue Ermita District Manila, National Capital Region 1004 Philippines. T=+63 (2) 523-8691. HC, D, E, SF=36,000. G=S, B, C, BJ, P, R, pai gow poker, and pontoon.

Casino Filipino Silahis, Grand Boulevard Hotel, 1990 Roxas Boulevard, Manila, National Capital Region 1004 Philippines. T=+63 (2) 525-7966 and +63 (2) 526-0122. HC, D, E, SF=27,700.
www.newpagcor.com or cf_sil.htm G=S, B, C, BJ, P, R, pai gow poker.

Casino Filipino Heritage, Heritage Hotel Manila, Roxas Boulevard, Pasay City 1300 Manila, National Capital Region 01000 Philippines. T=+63 (2) 854-8751. HC, E, SF=21,000. www.newpagcor.com or cf_her.htm
G=S, B, C, BJ, P, R, pai gow poker, and pontoon.

Japan: Dots the country with racecourses, expects to have Vegas-style casinos by 2010.

Central and South America (290)

Argentina, Peru, Costa Rica, Panama, Colombia, Uruguay, Ecuador, Chile, Nicaragua, Venezuela, Paraguay, Suriname, Belize, Honduras, El Salvador and Guatemala.

Most casinos in Central and South America are not large, however, I offer a taste of the "Latin casino scene" with these six countries.

1. Argentina:
Casino del Sol, Calle Rivadavia 57 Santiago del Estero, 4200 Argentina. T=+54 3858-423426. HN, SF=16,100. G=S, B, BJ, P, R.

Casino Central Mar del Plata, 2148 Maritimo Peralta Boulevard, Buenos Aires Mar del Plata, Buenos Aires 7600. T=+54 223-4957011. HN. G=S, C, BJ, R.

2. Chile:
Casino Vina del Mar, Avenido San Martin 199, Vina del Mar, Valparaiso 2520000 Chile. T=+56 32 500 600. HC, E. www.casino.cl or home.html G=S, B, BJ, C, P, CSP, R, boule, Crown and Anchor, and punto banco. Located 85 miles northwest of Santiago; a Pacific beach resort with a summer season.

3. Columbia:
Casino Caribe, Calle 52, 46-34, Medellin, Antioquia Colombia. T=+57 (4) 5124100. HC, SF=32,000. www.unidelca.com G=S, BJ, P, R.

4. Peru:
Majestic Casino and JW Marriott Hotel, Malecan de la Reserva 615 Miraflores, Lima Peru. T=+51 1 447 7000. HN=tables, HC, SF=1800. www.marriott.com or LIMDT G=S, B, BJ, CSP, C.

5. Costa Rica:
Presidente Hotel and Casino Fiesta, Avenida Central entre Calle 7 y Calle 9, San Jose 1017. T=Costa Rica. HC, SF=4400. . www.hotel-presidente.com G=S, BJ, P, R, pai gow poker.

Iraza Hotel Best Western and Casino Concorde, KM 3 Autopista Calle General, La Uruca, San Jose 1150 Costa Rica. T=+506 232 7910. HC, SF=4000. www.casinos-concorde.com. G=S, BJ, P, R, pai gow poker.

6. Panama:
Casino Majestic, Multicentro Paitilla Panama City, Panama. T: +507 215 5151 HC, SF=53,800. G=S, B, BJ, C, CSP, P, R.

Hotel El Panama and Fiesta Casino, Via Espana 111, Panama City, Panama. T=+507 215 9000. HC, SF=20,000. www.elpanama.com
HC, SF=53,800. G=S, B, BJ, P, R, race book.

Oceania (480)
Australia, New Zealand, Rèunion, New Caledonia, Solomon Islands, Vanuatu, and Northern Mariana Islands.

1. Australia
Over 400 casinos or sporting clubs and racecourses are located here. These three Australian casinos below offer the full complement of games, plus some Australian specialties, like Two Up, Manila Poker, and French boule. There are no entrance fees, and all are open 24 hours.

Star City, 80 Pyrmont Street, Sydney, New South Wales 2009 Australia. T=+61 2 9777 9000. HC, SF=104,000. www.starcity.com.au. G=S, B, BJ, C, P, R, sic bo.

Crown Entertainment Complex, 8 Whiteman Street, Melbourne, Victoria 3006, Australia. – T=+61 3 9292 5505 and +61 3 9292 8888. HC, SF=221,000. www.crownltd.com.au G=S, B, BJ, C, CSP, P, R, sic bo and pai gow poker.
There are 28 restaurants for your dining pleasure. These are two of the top ten casinos in the world, a must-see for visitors to the land of Oz.

Burswood Entertainment Complex, Great Eastern Highway Burswood,

Western Australia 6100, Australia. T=+61 8 9362 7777. HC, SF=75,000. www.burswood.com.au G=S, B, BJ, C, CSP, P, R, keno, and pai gow poker. Located on the Swan River near Perth, with impressive views and a pyramid-shaped hotel.

2. New Zealand
SkyCity Auckland, Corner of Federal Street and Victoria Street, Auckland, North Island 1001 New Zealand. T=+64 9 363-6000. HC, SF=71,000. www.skycity.co.nz G=S, B, BJ, CSP, P, R, pai gow poker, bingo, and tai sai. There are SkyCity casinos in Hamilton and Queenston, NZ.

Africa (175)

South Africa, Egypt, Kenya, Mauritius, Zimbabwe, Botswana, Equatorial Guinea, Tanzania, Morocco, Senegal, Tunisia, Cameroon, Namibia, Seychelles, Swaziland, Zambia, Ghana, Lesotho, Madagascar, Malawi, Mozambique, Nigeria, Sierra Leone, Benin, Comoros, Democratic Republic of the Congo, Djibouti, Gambia, Ivory Coast, Liberia, and Uganda.
    We visit casinos at the bottom, top, and middle of this continent.

1. South Africa:
Suncoast Casino and Entertainment World, 1 Battery Beach Road, Durban, Kwazulu-Natal 4359, South Africa. T=+27 31 328 3000. HC, D, SF=75,000. www.suncoastcasino.co.za G=S, BJ, C, R, punto banco.
    Located 32 miles west of Pretoria, this complex is the largest in South Africa, with a long list of amenities, including an entertainment center, golf course, tennis, and wildlife preserve. Lost City rooms offer a dreamlike, mythical African setting.

2) Egypt:
Inter Casino—Ramses Hilton Hotel, 1115 Comiche El Nile Street, Cairo, Al Quahirah, Egypt. T=+20 2 575 4125. HC. www.cairo-ramses.hilton.com G=S, BJ, R, punto banco.

Casino Semiramis—Inter-Continental Hotel, Hotel Semiramis Inter-Continental Corniche El Nile, Garden City Cairo, Al Quahirah 11511,

Egypt. T=+20 2 795 6724. HC. www.casinosaustria.com or cai_cas_casi-nos.aspx G=S, BJ, R, punto banco.

Cairo Marriott Hotel and Omar Khayyam Casino, Saraya El Gezira St. Zama-lek, Cairo, Al Quahirah Egypt. T=+20 2 735 8888. HC. www.marriott.com or CAIEG G=S, BJ, R, punto banco

4. Kenya:
Casino de Paradise at the Safari Park Hotel and Country Club, Thika Road, Nairobi, Kenya. T=+254 28 024 93. HN, HC, D, E, SF=15,000. G=S, B, BJ, R, chemin de fer, pontoon.

That completes our travels around the world in search of the finest casinos. I hope you enjoyed the adventure to these exotic, faraway places.

Appendix

A Review of the Basics and Key Strategies for Casino Games

Slots Quick Review and Tips

1) There are three types of slot machines: basic slots, progressives, and bonus slots, which include multi-lines and reels.
2) Basic Slots, or flat-tops, have a constant top jackpot payout.
3) Strategy: Look for single-payline and two-coin-maximum play to stretch your gambling bankroll.
4) Double or triple the payout with certain combinations—for example, Double or Triple Diamonds, or Blazing 7s.
5) Hit and Run: Five maximum spins for a return. In addition, take a maximum of five spins after a large jackpot win.
6) Progressives offer increasing jackpot payouts, dependent upon the amount of monies played through the linked bank or carousel of slots.
7) There are two levels of progressive jackpots, primary and secondary, with many graduated jackpots and pay-symbol possibilities.
8) A primary jackpot, displayed in large neon, is the top prize offered for a specific win combination.
9) Secondary jackpots are displayed on smaller screens and are hit more often, albeit lower payouts.
10) Progressives, online and off, are found in one casino or several participating casinos. After a progressive jackpot is hit, the meter automatically resets to the base jackpot amount.

11) Strategy: Before playing any single group of progressives, check out the primary and secondary jackpots, and then compare other progressives online and off for the best payouts relative to their starting amounts.

12) Look for progressive jackpots that are paid instantly.

13) Bonus slots: Multi-lines offer a "second-chance" video bonus screen round. Wild X Multipliers are bonus reel slots.

14) Bonus multilines: the screen shows at least twenty-five graphic symbols or characters, more than other slots. At least five or nine paylines and up to as many as fifty paylines may be played.

15) Bonus slots are available in penny to dollar denominations and up, online and off. They offer frequent payouts, usually every two to three spins.

16) Scatter-pay wild symbols pay anywhere on screen's crisscrossing pay lines.

17) Use the Help menu to determine the grid of various paylines and payouts for matching symbols.

18) Bonus Reel Slots or Wild X Multipliers feature multipliers, free spins, and possibly a fourth reel or top box. These bonus slots are popular with people who like to play traditional slots.

Strategy

- You do not have to play the maximum number of coins all the time, unlike with basic and progressive slots.
- Play one or two coins per line, activating all paylines, until you build some credits. Then the occasional maximum-coin spin is not a high risk.
- Play new bonus slot versions offered online and off whenever a new product has better payouts.

Video Poker Quick Tips

- Learn how to read pay schedules to understand the difference between full-pay and short-pay VP versions.
- Learn optimum strategy for each VP version before you play.
- Here are the top ten VP versions with the highest payout percentages, based on players' preferences and availability.

1) 10 or 4 Loose Deuces: 100.97 percent
2) 9/5 Deuces Wild: 100.76 percent
3) 7/5 Jokers Wild: 100.64 percent. Five of a kind pays 1,000. Quad pays 100. Kings + is the minimum payout.
4) 9/6 Double Double Jackpot Poker, also known as Aces and Faces: 100.35 percent
5) 10/7 Double Bonus: Two pair pays one coin = 100.17 percent
6) Pick 'Em Poker: 99.95 percent
7) 11/7 Triple Bonus Poker; the Kings+ minimum payout is 99.94 percent.
8) 9/6 Jacks+: two pair pays two coins = 99.54 percent
9) 8/5 Jacks+ Bonus: Two pair pays two coins = 99.17 percent.
10) 9/6 Double Double Bonus: 98.98 percent

The first two numbers reflect the payouts for a full house and flush as per a one-coin payout. For example, a 10/7 Bonus VP would pay ten coins for a full house and seven coins for a flush on a one-coin bet. The exceptions are Deuces Wild games; reflect the payouts for a straight flush and four of a kind as per a one-coin payout. These percentages are maintained with the maximum number of coins, full-pay schedules, and perfect strategy in play.

Strategy for three of the most popular VP versions:

<u>Jacks or Better (Jacks+)</u>
- A maximum-coin bet pays the winning hands multiplied by a factor of five, except the royal flush (4,000), which is an incentive to always play the maximum number of coins for each hand.
- 20 percent of hands dealt will be paying hands.
- 3 percent of the time, you will toss all five cards.
- The 6/5 VP payout is 72 percent. There's a big difference between full pay and this short-pay schedule.
- Keep a five-card winning hand unless one-card draw can make a straight or a royal flush.
- The ace is not the most important card; the king, queen, and jack are significant also, as they return your bet.

• Don't keep a kicker with a high pair.

Deuces Wild
• Strategy includes the prize for a secondary jackpot of four deuces.
• Approximately every 5,000 hands will be four deuces.
• Don't hold two pair, as the minimum payout is for three of a kind.
• Only one pair should be held.
• Almost 20 percent of the time, you will throw away all five cards.
• Never hold one card only, except a deuce.
• Never hold two cards unless they're a pair or a two-card royal draw, but not ace and king.
• Never hold just one other card with one, two, or three deuces.
• If there are no deuces, draw to an inside royal or straight flush because of the wild-card possibility.
• Jack to 7 offers the best straight potential.
• Play Double or Loose Deuces versions, where the secondary jackpot of four deuces pays double. Strategy change: Hold three deuces alone.
• Deuces Wild is a "roller-coaster ride" of a game. Bankroll fluctuations are expected.

Jokers Wild
• Uses a fifty-three-card deck to include one joker.
• Go for a straight flush when possible for the higher return with a wild card.
• Break up three of a kind for any four-card straight flush.
• Hold a lower pair instead of trying for an inside straight.
• Although this is a wild-card game, the pay for straights has been reduced from four to three coins.

Blackjack Quick Tips

1) Blackjack: Play "Dealer Must Draw to 16 and Stand on All 17s" tables.
2) Best: Single-deck tables, no double-down restrictions, resplitting and surrender allowed.
3) You only have to beat the dealer; you can win with a 13 or 14 hand and a dealer bust.

4) Master the hit and stand strategies and the true-count system for card counting.

5) Snag the third-base seat to survey all the cards on the table before your decision.

6) Watch for dealer tells. These signs can give away hands.

7) Don't take insurance.

8) Don't play blackjack at a table where the player's blackjack pays 6 to 5 or even money. Stick with the standard 3-to-2 payout.

9) Pass up blackjack tables that utilize a continuous-shuffling machine, where cards are returned to the shuffler after each round.

10) Quick-Tip Blackjack Strategy: Your Hand Against Dealer Upcard (D)

12 to 16: D stands on 2 to 6, hits on 7 to ace
17 to 21: D stands
10 or 11: D doubles down on 2 to 9
Soft 13 to 17: D hits except doubles down on 5 and 6
Soft 18 to 21: D stands except doubles down on soft 18 and 5 and 6
2,2; 3,3; 6,6; 7,7; 9,9: Player splits on 2 to 7 but stands on 9 and 9 against a 7.
5,5; 10,10: never split
8,8; ace, ace: always split

<u>Blackjack Terms</u>
Hard hand: A hand that does not include an ace. What you see on your two cards is your total count, such as $9 + 8 = 17$.
Soft hand: A hand that includes an ace in the first two cards dealt. It has two values, depending on whether you use the ace as a 1 or an 11. A 5 and an ace would be 6 or 16.
Stiff hand: A potential bust hand, such as a 13 or 14. Also, a hard 15 or 16.
Push: The same count as the dealer—a tie. No money is exchanged; you don't win or lose.
Burn cards: The number of cards the casino discards at the beginning of a new shuffle.
Multiple decks: Four or more decks played in a game, always dealt faceup.

Craps Quick Tips

1) Let's run through the numbers: 2, 3, and 12 are craps losers. 7 and 11—a "natural"—are winners.

2) Craps point numbers are 4, 5, 6, 8, 9, and 10 and these points must be repeated before a 7 is rolled.

3) When a player is handed the dice to throw, the first roll is called a "come-out," and a 7 or 11 immediately wins. The 2, 3, or 12 immediately loses.

4) If the player throws any of the other numbers—4, 5, 6, 8, 9, or 10—the player continues to throw until either that same point number is rolled again, in which case the player wins, or until a 7 is rolled, in which case the player loses.

5) Any other number has no significance to the pass-line wager. This explains why the 7 sometimes wins and sometimes loses. If it is thrown on the first roll, it wins. If it is thrown when the player tries to repeat his first-roll number, it loses and is called a 7-out.

Strategy Tips

- Keep pass-line and come bets to table minimum.
- Place odds bets, after the count is established, with as much as your bankroll will allow.
- This is where the money is made at the craps table.
- The odds bets are determined by a probability chart and are based on the thirty-six combinations a pair of dice can produce.
- For instance, the 7 can be rolled in six ways; this is the highest combination probability. The 6 and 8 can be rolled in five ways; the 5 and 9 can be rolled four ways, and the 4 and 10 can be rolled three ways each.
- Be sure to place the correct amount on odds bets (as illustrated below) or the casino will pay only even money.

6 and 8	6-to-5 odds	Pays $6 for every $5 wagered
5 and 9	3-to-2 odds	Pays $3 for every $2 wagered
4 and 10	2-to-1 odds	Pays $2 for every $1 wagered

- Therefore, placing the 6 and 8 is a good craps bet.
- Don't-pass and don't-come bets are excellent moves at a cold craps table.

Baccarat and Mini-Baccarat Quick Tips

1) You bet on either of the two hands to win—banker or player.
2) Additional wager is the tie bet.
3) The house edge is under 1.5 percent with strategic play.
4) All number cards, 2 through 9, count as their face value, or the number of pips on the card. All 10s and face cards count as 10. Aces count as 1.
5) No hand can be worth more than 9.
6) To quickly determine the value of a hand greater than 9, simply use the last digit of the total number—use 9 for 19, 0 for 20, 7 for 17, and so on.
7) An average shoe will deal about eighty-two hands

Strategy

- It is important to remember that no hand is too bad or too good to win initially, because the count can change with the third card, if one is required.
- One decision: Bet the player's or the banker's hand. You bet on either of the two hands to win.
- Avoid the tie bet as it has a 14 percent casino advantage.
- Mathematically, the banker hand has a slight edge over the player because of the third-card rules.
- Generally, for each show, the bank will win 38 times, the player 36 times, with 8 ties.
- The banker wins more because the bank stands on a 7, 8, or 9. The player stands on 6, 7, 8, or 9. The bank can draw on a 6, whereas the player cannot.
- However, the casinos have come up with a solution to this banker's advantage. They charge players a 5 percent commission each time they bet on the banker's hand and win.
- Card-counting basics are as follows: Cards more favorable to the banker's hand are 9,8,10,J,Q, and K, in order of strength. 4,3,2, and

5 are player-favorable cards. Ace, 6, and 8 are neutral—no favor for either hand.

- Bet on the player when there is a higher ratio of 2s through 5s in the deck; bet on the banker when there is a higher ratio of high cards in the deck.
- Try mini-baccarat, especially if you are a low-limit or novice player. The only difference between mini-baccarat and the full-size version of the game is that in mini-baccarat, all hands are dealt by a dealer—not the players.

Punto Banco Quick Tips

1) This game is similar to American baccarat with a few name and rule changes: the shoe is the sabot, the player is the punter, and the dealer is the croupier and is in charge of the game.
2) All cards are dealt faceup. The casino advantage is less than 2 percent.
3) A tie bet pays eight times the stake.
4) The first card brought out by the croupier and turned over determines the value of cards forthcoming before the first game of a new shoe begins. For example, a face card means that ten unturned cards are discarded; a 7 reads to seven unturned cards discarded, and so on. This method can make card counting difficult, so memorize which cards favor which hand.
5) Cards more favorable to the bank hand are 9,8,10,J,Q, and K, in order of strength; 4,3,2, and 5 are player-favorable cards; ace, 6, and 8 are neutral, not favoring either hand.

Chemin de Fer Quick Tips

1) You cannot bet on the banker or the player; you must be one or the other. Therefore, the casino has no direct involvement in the game. The bettors wager among themselves, as in U.S. poker.
2) The player who is acting as the banker places his or her bid (currency) in the middle of the table, and is responsible for covering all losing bets, while collecting winning bets.
3) Other players can now bet against all (banco) or any portion of this

money. The highest bidder is then dealt the player's hand.

4) There is no tie bet in this game, and no money changes hands when there is a tie.

5) The casino takes a 5 percent commission.

6) Third-card rules are different—bank-hand totals of 3 and 5 offer draw and stand options.

7) If you have the bankroll, the best strategy here is to be the banker.

Trente et Quarante (30/40) Quick Tips

1) Trente et Quarante, or 30/40, is played with six decks of cards and offers four bets: red, black, color, and inverse, all paying even money.

2) Aces are worth 1; face cards, 10; others are worth face value. Two hands are dealt; each row must exceed 30, but not go over 40.

3) The first row is black, the second red, and the winning point payout is the one nearer to 30, or the lower hand.

4) If the first card dealt in the first row is the same color as in the winning row, the color bet wins; if first card is of the opposite color, the inverse bet wins.

5) A tie is a push; however, if both rows equal 31, then bets lose only half the value.

6) The house advantage for this game is a low 1 percent. Additionally, you can purchase insurance that eliminates the half-loss for a tie of 31. It's your choice, as the house advantage is the same for any bet, but do take insurance to cut that edge a bit.

Roulette Quick Tips

1) Roulette is one of the more popular table games in U.S. casinos and is enjoyed worldwide.

2) Play single-zero wheels for a low casino edge of 2.63 percent. Double-zero roulette has a 5.26 percent house advantage.

3) In European roulette, the single zero is positioned between black 26 and red 32. Another plus is the en prison rule on even-money bets. When 0 comes up, your bet remains or is "captured" for the next spin. This en prison, or surrender, rule on even-money bets reduces

the casino's edge further, to 1.35 percent.

4) The five-number bet of 0, 00, 1, 2, and 3 has a large 7.89 percent casino advantage. Avoid this bet.

5) Make a series of pre-determined bets rather than betting "all over the table."

6) Sample Strategy: Start with forty chips; the $1 denomination is the least expensive way to go. Most tables require $5 minimum inside bets; you can qualify by placing five inside straight up bets. Use the same five numbers for a series of eight spins totaling your buy-in of forty chips. Choose your lucky numbers, based on favorite numbers or dates, and place a chip in the middle of each number each time. Any win will pay you 35–1, and two wins after eight spins brings in a profit. Try a repeat of eight spins or tuck away those winnings.

7) Spin for profits and don't forget progressive betting—upping your bet after each win.

Pai Gow Poker Quick Tips

1) The cards in pai gow poker are ranked like those in standard poker hands, except that one joker is found in the deck and can be played as an ace or the high card to finish a straight, flush, straight flush, or royal flush.

2) You must win both hands to win your bet. The house receives a commission on all winning hands. All players play against the banker.

3) Each player receives seven cards and must make two poker hands, the high hand made up of five cards, and the low hand, containing two cards.

4) The most important rule to remember is that the rank of the five-card high hand must be higher than that of the two-card low hand.

5) Once all the hands are set, the dealer will compare the players' hands with banker's hand for payouts.

6) If one of your hands is higher in rank than the dealer's and the other is lower, this is a tie and your bet remains on the layout. If the banker bests both of your hands, you lose your wager. If both hands are identical (a "copy"), the banker also wins.

7) The casino's advantage is about 2.8 percent, lowered to 2.5 percent

with perfect strategy.
8) A skillful banker can play an even game against the casino; therefore, try for the banker position as often as the casino allows.

Texas Hold 'Em Quick Tips

Currently, Texas Hold 'Em is the most popular poker game played world-wide.

1) The dealer deals out two cards, facedown and one at a time, to each player.
2) After all players receive their two cards, there is a round of betting where players can either call, raise, or fold. Checking is not allowed on this round.
3) The dealer then deals three cards faceup in the center of the table. Another round of betting begins.
4) There is fourth card placed faceup on the table, followed by a betting round.
5) The fifth and final card is placed faceup in the middle of the table; this is the final round of betting.
6) Players choose their best five-card hand from among seven cards. The winning hand is the highest poker hand.

Strategy
- Continue playing with strong starting cards if first two cards are two aces, two kings, or two queens.
- Other possible strong starting cards are A-K or A-Q suited.
- Fold if you have a pair lower than 7s.
- Look for cards in the flop lower than the rank of your pair.
- Strong hands with good possibilities require aggressive play by raising, and getting rid of players who could "draw out" (make bad hands into good hands).
- Only if you feel your hand has become second best should you fold.
- Marginal hands that may improve should only be played on the cheap, either by checking or with nominal bets.

- Holding a "lock hand," one likely to win (for example, a full house) requires a strategy to keep as many players in the pot as long as possible to build your win.
- Pick your times and players when bluffing. It is easier to bluff against one player and easier against good players, who respect the art, as opposed to weak players who stay in the pot forever.